PRINC

BUILDING A FUNCTIONAL RELATIONSHIP WITH JESUS CHRIST

Foreword by Sam Korankye Ankrah

Trilogy Christian Publishers
A Wholly Owned Subsidiary of Trinity Broadcasting Network
2442 Michelle Drive
Tustin, CA 92780
Copyright © 2024 by (Prince Sackey)
All Scripture quotations, unless otherwise noted, taken from THE HOLY BIBLE, NEW INTERNATIONAL VERSION®, NIV® Copyright © 1973, 1978, 1984, 2011 by Biblica, Inc.® Used by permission. All rights reserved worldwide.
All rights reserved, including the right to reproduce this book or portions thereof in any form whatsoever.
For information, address Trilogy Christian Publishing
Rights Department, 2442 Michelle Drive, Tustin, CA 92780.
Trilogy Christian Publishing/ TBN and colophon are trademarks of Trinity Broadcasting Network.
For information about special discounts for bulk purchases, please contact Trilogy Christian Publishing.

Trilogy Disclaimer: The views and content expressed in this book are those of the author and may not necessarily reflect the views and doctrine of Trilogy Christian Publishing or the Trinity Broadcasting Network.

10 9 8 7 6 5 4 3 2 1
Library of Congress Cataloging-in-Publication Data is available.
ISBN 979-8-89333-913-0
ISBN 979-8-89333-914-7 (ebook)

ACKNOWLEDGMENT

Throughout our earthly existence, from the moment of conception until our last breath, we come across numerous individuals who play significant roles in shaping our life's narrative. These individuals provide sagacity, erudition, comprehension, teachings, convictions, and heritage, molding our identity. Human beings do not exist in complete solitude; during our lives, we unavoidably encounter others who have a profound impact on us.

I deeply admire my mother, Phyllis V. Andoh, for nurturing and shaping me into the person I have become, just like Mary had a significant role in Jesus' life on earth. I would want to express my gratitude to my father, Mr. John Essel, who assumed the role of my father figure following the demise of my biological father, Mr. John K. Sackey. He imparted upon me the values that I really cherish. Angela South played a vital role in supporting us when we were asked by the Lord to go from Bronx, New York, where our ministry was thriving, to establish a new church in Texas. Her assistance was essential in accomplishing our heavenly mission. Mr. Cleanard Jarvis, my father-in-law, constructed our initial place of worship in Bronx, New York, with unwavering commitment.

I express my gratitude to Apostle Emmanuel Ketorley, hailing from Ghana, Bernard Baidoo, also from Ghana, and Martin Dzikpor. These three individuals, who have a covenant bond with me, have consistently provided unwavering support, encouragement, and motivation, propelling me towards progress. Pastor Etarigbenu Richard Onome, may the Lord bestow blessings upon you for your diligent efforts in assisting me with the organization of all the manuscripts. I express my profound gratitude to the family of Chosen and Royal Ministry for their unwavering prayers and support. Additionally, I extend my blessings to the numerous individuals whose names I am unable to enumerate in their entirety.

Finally, I would like to honor Apostle Sam Korankye Ankrah, my father in the Lord, and Bishop Alexander Adu Gyamfi, who have both been very impactful in my journey with God and ministry.

DEDICATION

This book is dedicated to God and my lovely wife, Shalaine Faith Sackey, for her unwavering encouragement and comprehensive assistance in ensuring the excellence of this book. I love you.

TABLE OF CONTENTS

Acknowledgment 5

Dedication. 7

Preface. 11

Endorsements 13

Foreword. 17

Chapter One: Eden to Exile 21

Chapter Two: Too Real to be True 33

Chapter Three: The Need for Light 45

Chapter Four: The Mystery of Being Born Again 57

Chapter Five: Building A Strong,
Functional Relationship 77

Chapter Six: The Third Person 117

Chapter Seven: Not Dash But A Marathon. 133

Chapter Eight: Nothing to Lose!. 147

About the Author. 153

Conclusion 155

PREFACE

I was consistently reminded of the profound truth that our relationship with Jesus Christ is not merely a religious obligation but a profoundly personal and transformative experience as I began the process of writing this book. This book was conceived as a means of assisting others in recognizing the beauty and profundity of a functional relationship with Christ, one that is not tainted by the misunderstandings of dread or remorse but, rather, is founded on the principles of love, grace, and truth. Delivering many from the legalistic mindset as thought all Jesus did was not enough. I delved into the core elements of our faith in these pages, commencing with the fall of man, a historical event that fundamentally altered the trajectory of human history. However, God's love for us remained unwavering, even in that moment of despair. The rescue point, the bridge that reconnected us to the compassionate embrace of our Creator, was Jesus Christ.

The Holy Spirit's role became a central personality as I further explored this relationship. The Holy Spirit is not merely a teacher or guide; He is a steadfast companion who assists us in navigating the intricacies of life, consistently directing us back to Christ. The Holy Spirit is the means by which we are able to establish and sustain a relationship with Jesus, particularly when we falter and fail. One of the most critical messages conveyed through this book is the significance of not attempting to distance oneself from God when one commits transgression.

I hope that as you peruse these chapters, you will not only develop a more profound comprehension of Jesus' identity but also experience a rekindled sense of His affection for you. May this book serve as an inspiration for you to pursue a relationship with Christ that is authentic, dynamic, and transformative. May you always remember that God's love is ever-present, prepared to lead you back to Him, regardless of where you are on your journey.

ENDORSEMENTS

"Are you struggling to improve your walk with God? Do you feel stuck in certain areas of your life as far as knowing and experiencing the real love and power of the Lord. Then I recommend this great book *Building a Functional Relationship with Jesus Christ* for you. You will be greatly enlightened and experience a great shift by the time you are done reading." – Ernestina Asante-Bediako, MD

"In my nineteen years of walking with God, I've come to understand the rules of engagement in the kingdom. *Building a Functional Relationship with Jesus Christ* is an inspired piece that will put your pieces together to establish your concrete useful relationship with Jesus Christ. Apostle Jeremiah Sackey is a man of God, and I have been privileged to be under his tutelage. The servant of God has availed himself once again to be inspired by the Holy Spirit to eradicate one of the major challenges in the body of Christ with this volume. This word-base, inspired, timeless masterpiece is a must read for those who are seeking intimate working relationship with Jesus Christ and also to rejuvenate those who are already in practical relationship with Jesus."

– Martin Dzikpor
King of The Jew Clothing Line (CEO)

"Just when you think of how to better yourself and your walk with God, He has directed this His humble servant, Apostle Prince J Sackey, to write this awesome book which has blessed me tremendously, and I know it will inspire this generation and generations to come to get back in seeking the Lord in spirit and in truth."

– Henry Agyekum Chemphe
Gospel Musician (Worship Artist)

"I love how the Holy Spirit has led Prince Jeremiah Sackey to bring clarity on how to walk with the Lord through this book. It gives a foundation and steps on how one can build a solid relationship with Christ. I am grateful for this read, and I am for certain that it will be blessing for the body of Christ in this end time."

– Pastor Othniel Hinckson
Spirit Life Church Dallas, Texas (Head Pastor)

"This is a must-read book. The Spirit of the Living God has given Apostle Sackey some clear and deep insight on the fundamentals of building a relationship with Christ Jesus and the benefits thereof."

– Bishop Alexander Adu Gyamfi
Bible Believing Tabernacle, Bronx, New York

"*Building a Functional Relationship with Jesus Christ* touched my heart in ways I didn't expect. In our journey as caregivers, whether tending to the physical needs of a newborn or nurturing the spiritual growth of a community, we must recognize the profound connection between our work and our relationship with God. At the Baby Nurse Specialist, we believe that every aspect of life, including our professional roles, is an opportunity to build a functional, thriving relationship with God. That is why we love this book and recommend it to anyone that needs spiritual guidance in their life. *Building a Functional Relationship with Jesus Christ* is a must-read for anyone seeking to deepen their faith and find peace in God's perfect timing."

– **Angela South**
Co-Founder of The Baby Nurse Specialist

"This book acts as a guiding light, helping believers refocus on the core message of the gospel, amidst a growing emphasis on legalistic interpretations that tend to eclipse the fundamental significance of Christ's sacrifice on the cross. It reveals the slight but important change that has caused many people to prioritize rules and rituals instead of recognizing the transformational impact of Christ's sacrifice. This work contains significant insights that enlighten readers about the perils of a religious belief system based on strict adherence to rules and regulations. It also emphasizes the emancipating fact that our connection with God is established not by our own efforts but through the completed actions of Christ. The book serves as a reminder to Christians that the essence of the gospel lies not in our actions but in the accomplishments of Christ, providing a route to a more profound and genuine faith."

**– Pastor Richard Onome Etarigbenu
of the Curriculum of the Spirit Ministries**

FOREWORD

Since the fall of man (Adam) in the book of Genesis, God has been looking for the pathway to return man into permanent union and fellowship, where his people will again occupy the position of their heirs and authority in God's plan for his creation. In this book *Building a Functional Relationship with Jesus Christ,* Apostle Prince J. Sackey sets out by revelation of God's holy word to unfold this divine pathway.

This book provides a thorough and comprehensive guide to establishing a functioning and close connection with Jesus Christ in a world filled with distractions and obstacles that frequently divert us from our real purpose. The narrative starts with the downfall of humankind, emphasizing the creation of a profound rift between mankind and God due to sin. However, it also unveils Jesus as the ultimate Savior, sent to reconcile and unite man and God. Salvation is not just portrayed as a means to avoid sin but as the fundamental embodiment of God's eternal and comprehensive love for humanity; a love that is dynamic, deliberate, and all-encompassing. This book delves into a comprehensive examination of the role of the Holy Spirit, illustrating how this Spirit aid consistently guides us towards a deeper connection with Christ, facilitating the healing of our fragmented existence and reinstating us to our original purpose. Crucially, the book emphasizes that sin should not push us away from God but rather draw us closer to Him, since the primary responsibility of the Holy Spirit is to guide us back, console us, and rejuvenate our souls with the illuminating power of Christ's redemptive love. This book is more than a script; it is a sincere invitation to encounter the entirety of God's love, understand the love, **and to live in the liberation that arises from completely surrendering one›s life to Jesus.**

Having pastored and mentored Apostle Prince for over two decades, I was amazed, drawn, and soaked into the store of wisdom and revelation encountered as I read the manuscript of this book. I have concluded from Apostle Prince's masterpiece that people may have their plans and ideas to the issues of life, but in the end, God's unquestionable purpose for his people, his creation, and the entire universe shall rule. This victory begins with the discovery of God's blueprint to salvation and union through Christ. Having this book *Building a Functional Relationship with Jesus Christ* written by Apostle Prince is the beginning divine assignment in fulfillment. I recommend it to everyone and any person irrespective of background, race, what you have been through, and what you are still going through; the answers to your questions are now in your hand. Read on.

–Foreward and recommendation
by Sam Korankye Ankrah, Apostle General
and Founder of Royalhouse Chapel Worldwide.

CHAPTER ONE
EDEN TO EXILE

"He came for your sin; stop running"

There was a young man by the name John. John's story begins in some peaceful suburb, the kind of place where Sunday mornings reverberate with soft hums of gospel hymns and rustling pages of well-worn Bibles. Born to devout Christian parents, John was brought up in a home where faith formed the bedrock of everyday life. He was taught, from an early age, to pray before his meals, to attend Sunday school, and to read scripture daily. His parents were pillars of the local church, respected for their staunch belief in Christ and their willingness to serve. John, as taught by his parents, did not view Christianity as a faith or belief system but as a way of life. From a boy, John worked deeply in his faith. He was a quick, enthusiastic young man who liked to be in the choir and to attend the youth group. His pastors and many in his church commented on his very evident purpose and character, saying he would probably one day be a pastor. From this, one might assume that John's life was on a steady and predictable course, one of service, devotion, and deepening faith.

But rarely is life as predictable as we think it to be.

That fateful afternoon brought tragedy to John's doorstep. It was one of those ordinary days; the sun brightly lit, the birds chirped, and John walked home from school. As he had meandered through a relatively secluded part of the neighborhood, he suddenly and violently was attacked by an older man who lured him to his house, claiming to be his father's friend, and thereafter assaulted John. The assault was swift, brutal, and it left John in tatters physically, emotionally, and spiritually. John did not know how to process what happened. Rape trauma left him very confused, isolated, and deeply ashamed. He could not tell his parents or anyone in the church. He was mortally afraid of their reactions, mortally afraid that they would condemn him or, worse still, blame him. The event was etched into his mind as a marker of dirtiness, one less worthy of the love and acceptance he had known all his life. John began to withdraw, his once-bright spirit now dimmed by some darkness from which he couldn't find an exit.

Months had cumulatively built a storm in John. He started questioning his identity, his religion, and his place with the world. Shame and confusion twisted into this thought: Maybe he was supposed to be different; maybe this was who he was supposed to be. Still in this place of vulnerability, John began searching for a world he had never known, very different from the one he had grown up in. John's search took him to places far from his church and family. He used to frequent clubs where he got introduced to a life that apparently gave him escape from his pain. The broken spirit was fed through the attention he got from various people in those places. It did not take John long to get involved in promiscuity and debauchery, where he became a stripper. It was a life at odds with every element of what he had been taught, but through the confusion and pain that created the haze he passed through felt like an element of acceptance, something which he direly needed at this point.

He still went to church every week, even with the huge upheaval in lifestyle. He would sit in the pews on Sunday mornings and hear the sermons, singing the hymns that everyone else did. On the face of it, John was the model Christian: faithful in service, consistent in attendance, and always ready to lend a helping hand. He went on leading youth groups, teaching Sunday school and engaging in other activities at the church. Outwardly, at least, his life was one of unwavering devotion to Christ. But inwardly, John knew something was grossly wrong. He was becoming ever more alienated from the man he was on Sundays to that man he was becoming the rest of the week. The more he tried to close the gap between his two lives, the greater a fake he felt. He could see admiration in the eyes of his fellow church members, hear their praises, but nothing brought him peace. It had been a double life he was living, and that inward cannibalizing had begun.

The real turnaround in John's life happened on that evening when he sat alone in his apartment. He had come home just that night from one of those countless evenings out, and looking at himself in a mirror, he saw a man he no longer recognized; with many, very flashy clothes, the mask over the organism, all this was grotesque. For the first time in years, he allowed himself to see what had been happening. He dropped down onto his knees and began to cry a deep, soul-rending cry welling up from the very bottom of his soul. It was then, in that utterly helpless state, that John came to understand how all these years he had been lying to himself more than to anybody else—and to God. He began to equate his outward righteous works with having a living, breathing relationship with Christ. He began to equate accolades from people with acceptance from God. He has been so focused on pretending to be faithful that he lost sight of what it really meant to follow Christ.

He lay down on the floor, crying. John groaned to God in desperation, confessing his sins, his doubts, and even his pains. He pleaded for forgiveness, healing, and renewal of purpose. He felt that, in that moment, something had begun to shift within him. It was not anything famous and prickly, overnight, and radical in terms of transformation; rather, it initiated him on a journey that would lead him back again to the Christ of his childhood, this time more profoundly authentic. It is not just John's story of sin and redemption; it's a warning to all of us about the dangers of a life merely lived in the appearances of religion. It is a story each one of us needs to answer concerning our own relationships with Christ. Are we way too much like John, content with the applause of other people, satisfied with appearances alone, or are we really desiring a practical, life-altering relationship with our Savior?

Now, remembering his story, take this to heart: How real is my relationship with Christ? What am I just following through on, and what is the Rock of my life? Wow, the story of John reminds us so strongly that Christ didn't call us to believe but to live it out in every part of life. Service will amount to nothing if our hearts are far from Him. Real faith just as John discovered is a matter of surrender: allowing ourselves to let go of the masks, the lies we tell ourselves, and sins that bind us, and embracing in return the transforming love of Christ.

The story of John also reminds us about the creation when God created Adam and placed him in the garden; in the garden was where man was kept; communion became the order of the day; the more man fellowshipped with God, the more he discovered the heart of God. It got to the time where Adam was now given the opportunity to name the creatures, and this was as a result of him being in that garden of Eden.

So God creates all the animals and the birds and brings them to Adam to see what he will

> *call them and "whatever the man called every living creature, that was its name".*
>
> **Genesis 2.19**

From the scripture above, it describes to us that from Eden God communicated with man, whatever man calls the creature, that was God's intention in terms of what he originally wants to call them. This was the privilege we were granted in Eden. It got to the point in time that God walked to the garden and desired fellowship from man and not just man desiring fellowship from God.

> *"And they heard the voice of the LORD God walking in the garden in the cool of the day: and Adam and his wife hid themselves from the presence of the LORD God amongst the trees of the garden".*
>
> **Genesis 3: 8**

The scripture above defined our relationship with God clearly. Thus, it was not just we desiring God, but it was God desiring that we come and have a time out with him. Also, remember we were created in God's image and after his likeness, as the scripture stated, replicating God's manner of love he has for us. Could this be true love? If this is true love, why then did he allow man to fall? What then is the essence of this relationship? These questions ring in our hearts every now and then about how a God who claimed he loved us could allow us take a journey from Eden to Exile? Before answers can be given, it becomes imperative that clarity is brought as touching the concept of a relationship.

Relationship by the Oxford, dictionary is defined as the way in which two or more concepts, objects, or people are connected or the state of being connected. It is also the state of being connected by blood or marriage. For example, they can trace their relationship to a common ancestor, or they are connected through a common faith. It can also be away in which two or more people or groups regard and behave towards each other. So by these examples and definitions, we can argue that relationship involves two or more people or objects that are connected to or with each other. Examples of relationships are secular relationships, marriage, family, romantic, social, communities, and even nations. Relationship can also be functional or non-functional, depending on the dynamics and genuineness behind such a relationship. For example, in a practical functional relationship, the two parties shall communicate freely and genuinely be committed to the growth and well-being of the other person. There exists mutual respect, trust, and a sense of purpose. A relationship can even then work superficially in terms of getting through daily interactions and meeting expectations of society, with little depth or connection. For instance, it could be held together by habit, obligation, or fear of change and not by some fundamentally emotional tie that binds the parties.

Another keyword to be considered is the word **functional.** This is simply because you can have a non-functional relationship, just as stated above, which does not serve any purpose and can be time consuming and waste of resources, which eventually will collapse because of many factors. Anything that is not functional, be it relationship, a car, shoe, house etc., is eventually discarded or thrown away. The word **functional** can be defined as having a special activity, purpose, or task relating to the way in which something works or operates. We understand that everything established, made or created has a function, the reason or purpose for which it was made, and it must be useful for that reason in order to serve its function. A clear example could be the car is very beautiful, but it has no space, and the trunk is little. It means it cannot be used for bigger transportation purpose. So, a functional relationship is a relationship between two or more people or group that is healthy and serving its true purpose, for which it was established. For a relationship to be functional and healthy, there must be honesty, humility, trust, unity, balance of power, respect, good communication, sharing of ideas and thoughts without fear of retribution or retaliation, and desire to grow. It goes beyond just confessions or words but by good actions like emotional, intellectual, spiritual, soulish, or physical connections and attractions. You connect to each other to form a relationship through common values, goals, and a genuine understanding of each other.

> *"Can two walk together except they be agreed?"*
>
> **Amos 3:3**

With the above scripture, we are made to understand that, without agreement, two people cannot walk together. Where there is discord or no unity, even the very best of relationships will fail. And of course, there is the most vital ingredient that cannot be taken away from any functional relationship, which is **love**. People cannot come together in harmony to fulfill a purpose or destiny if there is no genuine love. Without genuine love, the relationship will collapse when difficulty arises. So the Bible encourages us in 1 Corinthians 16:14 "to let all your things be done with love." Here Apostle Paul postulated that, even our obedience and services to Christ must be done in love and not forced.

God's act of creation, in relation to man, reflects the idea of true love based upon the freedom of choice characteristic of Divine love. God Himself says in one of the most essential texts written in Genesis 1:27 that He created man in His image and left a right of free choice for man. Love is not something that can be coerced or compelled but given and received freely. That is why God allowed man to fall, manifested in Genesis 3, where free will was exercised by Adam and Eve in the disobedience of God. God did not fail as a loving God by allowing them to choose; rather, He affirmed that He really is a loving God. God gave humans free will; therefore, He desires a meaningful love relationship with creation, not in any way forcing or demanding it through human will.

Even provided before man's fall, God's redemptive

plan was at the very heart of this relationship. That God chose us in Christ before the foundation of the world for the purpose of our being holy and blameless in His sight is made plain in Ephesians 1:4-5. Yes, humankind did fall. But God's love never fell. He just allowed the fall to let the world know how far He loves (a pursuing, redeeming, and restoring love). From the journey right from Eden to exile, God demonstrates through the sacrifice of Jesus Christ the longing for man's reconciliation with Him, as it is said in John 3:16. This was the ultimate act of love, whereby God showed that true love does not betray but is patient, offering a way back into a renewed relationship with Himself. At the very core of God's relationship with man lay the foundation of love once just, yet merciful, giving free will but extending a way of redemption, nonetheless. Thus, salvation became a display of God's love to mankind.

To wrap up this chapter, it becomes imperative that you give honest reviews as to your life. I will love you to be sincere to yourself as touching these questions as it will serve as a form of evaluation towards helping you discover the state of your relationship with Christ.

1. Have you accepted Jesus into your life genuinely?

2. Do you have a personal prayer time and fellowship with him?

3. Do you live a life in response to his love?

4. Are you sure your current standard of living was what Grace came to purchase?

Think upon these! If you find any of these questions difficult to answer or a part in your heart disproves it, it is expedient that you take a turn and return back to him. As we delve through the next chapter, you will be opened up to the truth that is TOO REAL TO BE TRUE.

CHAPTER TWO
TOO REAL TO BE TRUE

"Real love can be too perfect to be true"

I had the privilege to live in one of the most dangerous communities when I arrived here in the United States. I learned a great deal of a practical lesson, which to date has helped me take my relationship with Christ very seriously. On this block that I lived, which was characterized by violence and criminal activities, I realized that there was this particular guy who was young and seen as a gang leader. He was so much respected by all, whether you were a law-abiding citizen or a part of his gang or other group. The name of this particular guy rang bells and feelings of fear, anxiety, and depression when it was mentioned or when you saw him approaching. Nobody wanted any problems with him or anything connected to him like family and friends. There were times you would think the cops around the block were afraid of him.

Many times when guys were sitting down the block and his girlfriend was passing by, everybody looked away, regardless of how attractive she looked or revealing her dressing was. Families living in the community would immediately advise their visitors or guest to be careful about this guy and warned their boys not to try to talk to that particular girl of the gang leader. His name commanded respect, fear, power, loyalty to name a few. On the other hand, others wanted to be on his good side for covering, while other girls would throw themselves at him because they wanted the respect the other girl had hanging out with him. Take some seconds to imagine how everyone around him was being terrified to approach a girl because of the young man's jealousy. His influence, on the other hand, made everyone want to identify with him. This is just a mortal man! How about the King of Glory?

I took time to share the story to get you to understand how fearful and intimidating you will be to demons, witches, and the kingdom of darkness when you get to know the true Jesus whom all power belongs too. Imagine becoming His bride; you will automatically be feared, respected, saluted, and no one will dare cross your lines. This means sickness, diseases, demonic attacks like anxiety, depression, and suicidal thoughts will be a thing of the past. The thing is, not many people have clear understanding of the benefits of being in an intimate relationship with the son of the most powerful and glorious King of kings. Remember, though he had limited power and under authority, the cops could take him away anytime, and even so, nobody would testify against him. David says it better:

> "Blessed be the Lord who daily loads us with benefits, the God of our salvation! Selah".
>
> **Psalms 68:19**

Now I will move on to tell you about Jesus, the man waiting for your serious commitment to put his name on you and mark you as His. This scripture sends chills down my spine as a believer:

> "I will send my fear (terror) before you, I will cause confusion among all the people to whom you come and will make all your enemies turn their backs to you".
>
> **Exodus 23:27**

With this scripture above in relation to the testimonial story above, I pray you are getting a clearer picture and your spirit is stirred up to review your relationship with Jesus and make it your priority. God indeed protects His children, and His angels are ever-ready and present to fight for you.

> "Therefore he sent horses and chariots and a great army there, and they came by night and surrounded the city. And when the servant of the man of God arose early and went out, there was an army, surrounding the city with horses and chariots. And his servant said to him, 'Alas, my master! What shall we do?' So he answered, 'Do not fear, for those who are with us are more than those

who are with them.' And Elisha prayed, and said, 'Lord, I pray, open his eyes that he may see.' Then the Lord opened the eyes of the young man, and he saw. And behold, the mountain was **full of horses and chariots of fire all around Elisha***".*

2 Kings 6:14-17

We are always surrounded by numerous angels who are working to lead, protect help us in every area of our life. Now to get one of the most important questions of this book:

WHO IS JESUS?

"In the beginning was the word and the word was with God and the word was God. The same was in the beginning with God, all things were made by Him, and without Him was not anything made that was made, in Him was life, and the life was the light of man and the light shineth in darkness and the darkness comprehended it not".

John 1:1-5

With this scripture above, we can clearly tell that Jesus is the Son of God. He is the creative power of God. You see, God created the whole world and everything in it with words. In Genesis 1, He started off creation by saying in words, "Let there be light," and immediately there was an expression of those words in the form of light, and from there, everything else was created. Can you now imagine the amount of power that was at play? This is good news for you reading this right now. It means Jesus didn't lose that power, that creative ability to create in you new things like a liver, heart, kidneys, sight, and cause your dry bones to rise again.

The love Christ holds for humanity is just too deep a mystery that no length of human understanding can ever exhaust. It is transcendental, timeless, boundless, and spaceless, so deep and so pure that it seems too perfect to be true. Yet, it is this very love that forms the foundation of the Christian faith: that same love poured out for all humanity in the life, death, and resurrection of Jesus Christ. And to know even a little of this love brings one already face to face with a love that is not only undeserved but overwhelming, something that gets one down to one's knees in awe and thankfulness. First, God created heaven and earth and then man in His image and likeness. That is according to Genesis 1:27, "So God created man in His own image, in the image of God He created him; male and female He created them." This creation act gave mankind singular dignity and honor above all other creatures. Man was created to live in perfect harmony with God, to walk with Him in the closest fellowship possible, and through all that man did, to reflect His glory. In Eden, within the garden, there was to be a place to know perfect peace and joy: paradise—a place where man and woman would not know pain or suffering or separation from their Creator. It was a relationship built on love, a mutual, pure, and full one.

But the perfect relationship was broken when Adam and Eve heeded the words of the serpent, which led to their decision to disobey God. The tragic fall of man is described in Genesis 3, whereby sin came into the world through their disobedience. Everything changed in that instant. The unbroken fellowship between God and man was broken, and with it, the curse of sin and death was brought forth. Then man was cast out of Eden, away from God's presence, and the world was plunged into darkness. That first sin made devastating consequences not only for Adam and Eve but for the whole of humanity.

> *"Therefore, just as one man's sin entered into the world, and death through sin, thus to all men death passed, because all sinned".*
> **Rom 5:12**

There yawned the great gulf that separated man from God—the sin-barrier which no works of man could span. And yet, even now, amidst the tragedy, the love of God for humanity does not change. Though it grieved His heart to see them go astray, He did not abandon them unto their fate. In its stead, He initiated a divine plan of redemption that should work its way through history until it consummated in the greatest act of love the world has ever known. It wasn't conceived from the standpoint of duty or obligation.

It was blood-bought, incomprehensible love that is so perfect that nothing could get in the way to reclaim what was lost. That love came into its fullest expression in the Person of Jesus Christ.

At the fullness of time, God sent out His only Son into the world, not as an anointed king or mighty ruler but as a humble servant. Now, Philippians 2:6-8 gives this description of the great humility: "Who, being in very nature God, did not consider equality with God something to be used to His own advantage; rather, He made Himself nothing by taking the very nature of a servant, being made in human likeness. And being found in appearance as a man, He humbled Himself by becoming obedient to death; even death on a cross!" The One who spoke all-stars into existence, holds everything together by the power of His word, chose to humble Himself and become a man. He did not think of His privileged position as God but laid that all aside and took on the frailty and limitation of human flesh. Thus was the King of kings made a servant, not because He had to be but because His love for humanity was such that He could do nothing less.

In many respects, Jesus showed this love throughout His earthly ministry. He healed the sick, gave sight to the blind, and raised the dead. He further continued his touch to the outcasts, the sinful, and the brokenhearted, those whom society rejected and condemned. It was his fingers that touched lepers, letting them know they were not beyond the reach of his love. He washed away the sins of prostitutes and tax collectors, those whom society wrote off, and gave them a fresh start and a place in the coming kingdom of God. And He taught with authority, giving articulation to the heart of the Father toward a people who had long forgotten what it is to be really loved. In every word He spoke and every action He did, Jesus revealed God's perfect love because it is patient, kind, and sacrificial. It was a love that searched out the lost, the broken, and the weary and gave them hope, healing, and redemption.

The greatest demonstration of His love was yet to come. Jesus knew full well that He was born not only to teach or to heal but to eventually lay His life in sacrifice for the sins of the world. As John 15:13 declares, "Greater love has no one than this that someone lay down his life for his friends." And so did he with Jesus. It is in the Garden of Gethsemane, while He was praying in agony, knowing what awaited Him, that He submits to the Father's will out of love for us:

> *"Father, if You are willing, take this cup from Me; yet not My will but Yours be done".*
> **Luke 22:42**

Yet, it was within his grasp to summon legions of angels to liberate him; nonetheless, he went to the cross, for he knew that to be the only way by which the chasm dug between God and man because of sin could be bridged. The guiltless Son of God was betrayed, arrested, and then tried in a mockery of justice. He was beaten, spat upon, and mocked by those whom He came to save. Then a crown of thorns was placed on His head, and He was scourged until His back was a bloody mess. Yet He opened not His mouth. He was taken away with the usual victim, led to the slaughter like a lamb. Then He Himself had to carry His cross where He was to be executed: Golgotha, or the place of the skull. There He was nailed to the cross, piercing iron spikes through His hands and feet, and elevated before everybody's eyes. He did something great as He hung there on the cross, gasping for every breath in pain beyond comprehension. Instead of cursing those who crucified Him, He prayed for them, saying,

> *"Father, forgive them, for they do not know what they do".*
> **Luke 23:34**

Even on that day of His greatest suffering, even at that very moment, He loved them. And then, in a loud voice, He cried out, "It is finished." With these words, the work of redemption was complete. The debt of sin had been paid in full and the way opened for all who believe to be reconciled to God. The love of Christ was manifested full and perfect at that moment. He had taken upon Himself the sins of the world: the sins of every man, woman, and child, past, present, and future. He bore the whole weight of the wrath of God upon Himself, the chastisement that was due to us, that we might be spared. 2 Corinthians 5:21 says, "God made Him who had no sin to be sin for us;

in Him, we have the righteousness of God." This is the great exchange; our Lord gave us His righteousness, and in return, He carried our sin and died our death. It is a love so perfect, so undeserved, that it seems too good to be true.

Yet the story has more to tell. In dying, He destroyed our death, and rising He restored our life. In the third day, this Jesus arose from the dead and triumphed over sin, death, and the grave. Indeed, His rising is the last proof of His love and power. No more room for doubt that Love was defeated. He showed that He truly has overcome the forces of darkness so that life might be brought into this dying world. Romans 8:38-39 assures, "For I am convinced that neither death nor life, neither angels nor demons, neither the present nor the future, nor any powers, neither height nor depth, nor anything else in all creation, will be able to separate us from the love of God that is in Christ Jesus our Lord." Christ's love is indestructible, eternal, and unchangeable. His love is running towards us when we're running away, picking us up at our broken places, giving hope when all seems lost.

This love is not abstract and distant; it is very personal and intimate, an offer of love to each one of us. The love of Christ is there for all of us at all times, whatever may be our background or our deeds. It is the very love of Christ calling us out from the darkness into His very bright light. It is that love, bringing renewal in the mind and the heart, changing us into a new creation in Christ that answers the alienation. Yes, a love that answers the deepest groaning of our souls, love that gives peace, happiness, satisfaction beyond something that cannot be found in this world.

And this very love calls for a response. He has given all for us: His life, His blood, His very self, and He demands our answer that we receive His great love, open our hearts for Him, and follow Him. This is not a burden but, rather, a privilege, since in following after the Almighty are the true meaning and purpose of our beings. Jesus said, "Come unto me, all ye that labor and are heavy-laden, and I will give you rest." He calls us to come to Him just as we are, with all our sins, fears, and doubts, and find in Him that rest and peace which our poor hearts so much need.

Indeed, the love of Christ is too perfect to be true, and yet it is true. Never in the history of the world was human affection so proven beyond a shadow of a doubt by the cross and the empty tomb to indeed be the truest, most real thing in all the universe. It is one that continues to seek us out, continues to draw us close, and continues to make us whole. A love that is there for everyone that wants it, a love that shall never fade nor fail, never let us go. A love upon which we must meditate to be brought to tears, but not of sorrow—tears of thankfulness, awe, and wonder. A love that surpasses all loves that we can even think of, far beyond what we can dream and be hopeful of. In that love, we find our real home, our true identity, and our real destiny. And may we receive with open hearts all that, and let it transform us from the inside out, that we will lend our lives to reveal the glory of the One who loved us and led

Himself up for us.

Welcome to Love! Yes it is true! He did everything because all he wants you to do is just to believe he did it (faith)!

CHAPTER THREE
THE NEED FOR LIGHT

*"I owe him everything
when he laid down everything."*

You can bind a man, blindfold him, and cast him into the darkest and deepest pit with nobody around to talk to, and he will still be able to communicate with the pit fully covered. I know you are asking how?

The thing is every man who is alive is not only alive in the flesh but possesses a soul and spirit which enables him to communicate with spiritual entities, even when he is alone. Often times people who are going through a mental crisis will see that they have voices in their head, urging them to kill, steal, destroy or even take their own life. Those voices are spiritual forces, depending on the person who he is connected to that influence and try to manipulate their decision making and judgments. These are the forces that influence men on how to even live their lives and behave. One man's spirit and soul can house over 6000+ demonic spirits, which can easily influence his decision-making and cause him to harm himself and other people. There is no human without a spirit controlling him. It is either the spirit of God or that of the devil. As we read in the Bible:

> *"And they arrived at the country of the Gadarenes, which is over against Galilee. And when he went forth to land, there met him out of the city a certain man, which had devils long time, and ware no clothes, neither abode in any house, but in the tombs. When he saw Jesus, he cried out, and fell down before him, and with a loud voice said, what have I to do with thee, Jesus, thou Son of God most high? I beseech thee, torment me not. (For he had commanded the unclean spirit to come out of the man). For oftentimes it had caught him: and he was kept bound with chains and in fetters; and he brake the bands and was driven of the devil into the wilderness. And Jesus asked him, saying, what is thy name? And he said, Legion: because many devils were entered into him".*
> **Luke 8:26-30**

I highlighted the last sentence for you to pay particular attention to it. Legion means 6000+ because that was a term used to quantify a group of Roman soldiers in early days. So even though he was one man, he was in touch with 6000+ demonic spirits, and that was the source of his confusion in his head, soul, and spirit which resulted in madness and him living at the cemetery instead of a home and being bound in chains because he was capable of harming himself and others. Now you may be tempted to say, "I will not invite any spirits in me" and that you want to mind your business and don't want religion or God nor Satan. The truth here is that spirits sometimes don't even need an invitation. They just show up to a man, and when you are not filled with any spirit, they will occupy you and use you for whatever purpose they want based on their nature. How do I know spirits can invite themselves or invade your life when you are empty and not guarded?

"Then Jesus was led up by the Spirit into the wilderness to be tempted by the devil. And when He had fasted forty days and forty nights, afterward He was hungry. Now when the tempter came to Him, he said, 'If You are the Son of God, command that these stones become bread.' But He answered and said, 'It is written, "Man shall not live by bread alone, but by every word that proceeds from the mouth of God."' Then the devil took Him up into the holy city, set Him on the pinnacle of the temple, and said to Him, 'If You are the Son of God, throw Yourself down. For it is written: "He shall give His angels charge over you," and "In *their* hands they shall bear you up, Lest you dash your foot against a stone."' Jesus said to him, 'It is written again, "You shall not [a]tempt the Lord your God."' Again, the devil took Him up on an exceedingly high mountain, and showed Him all the kingdoms of the world and their glory. And he said to Him, 'All these things I will give You if You will fall down and worship me.' Then Jesus said to him, 'Away with you, Satan! For it is written, "You shall worship the Lord your God, and Him only you shall serve."' Then the devil left Him, and behold, angels came and ministered to Him" (Matthew 4:1-11).

We read that Jesus was alone for 40 days and nights fasting, and yet when He was done, the Satan came to tempt Him by trying to cause Him to turn stone into bread, throw Himself from the mountain to see if God will catch Him, and the final attempt was asking Jesus to bow down to him in exchange for all the kingdoms of the world. So, here we realize all these conversations going on with Jesus, triumphing over the devil because He had the Spirit of God in Him, and He had just finished performing spiritual exercises like prayers and fasting. You cannot overcome Satan with Satan or darkness with darkness but, rather, light. Go with me as I show you why we need a relationship and the three most important relationships a man need.

> *"And the LORD God said, It is not good that the man should be alone; I will make him an help meet for him".*
>
> **Genesis 2:18**

This verse mentioned above, as simple as it may sound, forms the basis of a man's needs to interact and be with other people. God never wanted man to be alone because loneliness is something that makes people feel empty, and it can open

THE NEED FOR LIGHT

up doors for negative thoughts and energies. Nobody dwells in a vacuum, and there are certain situations, when you are going through them, you realize you need someone to talk to or a shoulder to lean on. For example, when you are sick and admitted in the hospital. You would love company that can give you words of encouragement and hope, and just by putting a smile on your face, you begin to feel better. As the Bible says in Proverbs 27:17, "Iron sharpeneth iron; so a man sharpeneth the countenance of his friend." Now we are going to dive deeper and see why we need relationships and the three most important relationships a man need. The three most important relationships that complete the life of a man are:

- **Relationship with God,**
- **Relationship with yourself, and**
- **Relationship with others (family, marriage, friends, etc.)**

Now I will help you understand these three types of relationships and how important they are for you.

RELATIONSHIP WITH GOD

Before God created man, He had already prepared a place for him, which had everything a man would need and more, plus the most important thing which was the presence of God. Eden was a place where God positioned man, and He came to visit man from time to time. God never intended for man to be isolated from Him. He wanted to be in touch and commune with man on a daily basis. So the first greatest commandment as Jesus spoke in Matthew 22:37-38 says, "Thou shalt love the Lord thy God with all thy heart, and with all thy soul, and with all thy mind. This is the first and great commandment." This means that before men can decide to build any other relationship, His first love as God his creator must be well established and blooming. The problem is most people know and accept that there's a God, but their love for Him is not complete. They either only acknowledge His existence or they love Him with some part of them to some extent. But we are required to love Him with all of us.

ALL OF YOU MUST LOVE ALL OF GOD.

A man who truly loves God submits under his leadership and authority. And any man who can submit to authority is a submissive man who is able to humble himself to love and serve others. People who are often times rebellious against God cannot build a strong, healthy, and functional relationship where there is genuine love, respect, understanding, obedience, forbearance, forgiveness, and self-denial. Loving God requires obedience, and if a man can comply with the commandments and ordinances of God, he can function properly to relate to others well as the Bible commands. So we noticed that it was when man rebelled against God that all problems began and we were driven out of the presence of God. The guilt of Adam after the rebellion made him to even hide from God when God visited:

> *"And they heard the voice of the LORD God walking in the garden in the cool of the day: and Adam and his wife hid themselves from the presence of the LORD God amongst the trees of the garden. And the LORD God called unto Adam, and said unto him, 'Where art thou?' And he said, 'I heard thy voice in the garden, and I was afraid, because I was naked and I hid myself'".*
> **Genesis 3:8-10**

This means that any man that can hide or attempt to hide from God who is a Spirit and can see everything and be everywhere at the same time will surely not be honest to a fellow man, be it a brother, friend, spouse, business partner, etc. It means that men lack accountability and honesty, which is a great virtue for any relationship to be healthy and bloom. Also, during creation, the Bible says that God had to breathe into man His Spirit in order for men to become a living soul.

> *"And the LORD God formed man of the dust of the ground, and breathed into his nostrils the breath of life; and man became a living soul".*
> **Genesis 2:7**

This is where the distinction between man and other

creations are made. Man is made up of a body, soul, and spirit. This puts men in a position where, without other human contacts, men can still communicate and form relationships. The body of man interacts with other fleshly bodies (other men and creations). Then we have the **Soul,** which is the immaterial part of a man, which is the emotions of a person where feelings, desires, and affections are expressed. The soul forms the character or the substance of a person. The word used for soul in the Old Testament is *nepes*, and in the Greek New Testament language, it is *psyche*. So the soul gives life to the body, so, therefore, the body plus breath equals life. The **Spirit** aspect of a man is open to interactions with other spirits, consciously, subconsciously, and unconsciously, depending on the state of the mind of the man. While our soul speaks to us through our imaginations, mind, heart, will, dreams, desires, and decision-making or thinking, and our life experiences, our spirit connects us to the Spirit of God, who is the Holy Spirit, or other negative spirits known as demonic spirits, if you are not connected to God. It is important to know that your spirit can never be alone or isolated. It will always be in touch to either the Spirit of God or a negative spirit because it is open to interactions. Spirits interact with our spirit and soul to influence our thoughts, decision making and to influence our life and the way we live and interact with others. As the scripture says, "God is a Spirit: and they that worship Him must worship him in spirit and in truth in John 4:24. And so is the devil also busy moving to and fro seeking whom he may devour, so the Bible says in 1 Peter 5:8, "Be sober, be vigilant; because your adversary the devil, as a roaring lion, walketh about, seeking whom he may devour." The choice is always in your hands in order to shut the door to the opposing spirits.

RELATIONSHIP WITH YOURSELF

The level of love and respect you have for yourself will determine how much you can love others and treat them well. You cannot hate yourself and love others well. This is why it is very important to know how to love yourself, treat yourself well, groom yourself, respect and take good care of yourself. If you are not physically, emotionally, mentally, soulishly, spiritually well, then you cannot be beneficial to others as you cannot function well for yourself. Now you may be asking if this is scriptural. Jesus spoke and said the second great commandment is,

> *"Thou shalt love thy neighbor as thyself. On these two commandments hang all the law and the prophets".*
> **Matthew 22:39-40**

Notice that Jesus said "as thyself." It means you cannot love your neighbor more than yourself. The way you feel about yourself most likely will show when you encounter people and deal with them, especially when there is a problem. Someone who is miserable and angry will always project those type of attitudes and energies on others when dealing with them. So this means self-care is very important in life, and you can build yourself up really well by loving the Lord and allowing his word to build you up through His Spirit. When you engage in daily spiritual practices like reading and meditation on the word of God, praying and obeying the Word, the Holy Spirit will flow through you and remove all the negative thoughts and images you have about yourself and help you to build a positive self-image and strong spirit. Sometimes, as we grow up, we are affected by our environment, negative words spoken to us, abuse, which can come through the form of rape or physical attacks, disappointments, and failures in certain areas, and our lives can give us negative image and attitude. As the word of God says in Romans 12:2, "And be not conformed to this world: but be ye transformed by the renewing of your mind, that ye may prove what is that good, and acceptable, and perfect, will of God." The word of God coupled with prayers will build your faith and give you a quality life, full of joy, peace, and pure love, which you can then transmit to others.

RELATIONSHIP WITH OTHERS/NEIGHBORS

> *"And as ye would that men should do to you, do ye also to them likewise".*
>
> **Luke 6:31**

This commandment above I believe is very straightforward. Too many times we expect our spouses, families, friends at work, church, etc. to give us the best and special treatment. But in order to be the sweetheart of others, you must make them feel as though they are your sweetheart as well. Also, not all the time people treat you right in return, but the focus is always on you doing it first and leaving the rest to God. In loving and building relationship with others, you must be willing to be patient, kind, honest, not envious, not boastful, not proud, and not jealous. You must not dishonor others, not self-seek, not be easily angered; you must not keep record of wrongs. You must not delight in evil but rejoice with the truth. You must be willing to protect others always, trust always, hope always, and persevere.

> *"Love suffers long and is kind; love does not envy; love does not parade itself, is not puffed up; does not behave rudely, does not seek its own, is not provoked, [b]thinks no evil; does not rejoice in iniquity, but rejoices in the truth; bears all things, believes all things, hopes all things, endures all things".*
> **1 Corinthians 13:4-7**

If you are self-centered, then you cannot build a strong, healthy relationship with others, and people will not often times enjoy being around you. *Look for ways to help build others, and others will build you up as well.*

In conclusion if you want to know what spirit you are in relationship with and is ruling over you, then pay attention to your thoughts and emotions. If they are negative like lust, suicide, anger, jealousy, bitterness, misery, etc., then it is the devil at work in you, and if it is love, peace, joy, happiness, contentment, etc., then it is the Spirit of the Lord. Loving, caring, and treating yourself so well makes you treat others better and others treating you better and respecting you is a reflection of what you give.

CHAPTER FOUR
THE MYSTERY OF BEING BORN AGAIN

"Being born again doesn't make you less!"

The process of being a born-again Christian is a very great mystery that only the Spirit of the Lord can unravel to you, and it is the most beautiful moment in a man's life when it happens. This is a spiritual moment where a man in our fallen state gets connected back to God through faith and grace. Nicodemus came to Jesus at night to inquire about who Jesus is, His works, personality, and how much He is connected to God, who Nicodemus, a great teacher of the Word, believed he knew very well. He knew the word of God but was lacking the Spirit that brings understanding and power. First, the meaning of his name: Nicodemus means "victory of the people"; interestingly enough, the one who will make his name complete and functional was in front of him, and he could not perceive it. He was very great, successful and admired by his people, and many times, it is our success that makes us feel like we are sufficient and independent. We naturally want to lead and not be seen by our followers as a follower. His encounter with Jesus at the beginning of Jesus' ministry brought more light and understanding about faith, rebirth, and salvation. In John 3:1-21, he is introduced as there was a man of the Pharisees named Nicodemus, a ruler of the Jews. He thought Jesus was from God but was not the Messiah, and he was amazed about the works of Jesus. After his questioning of who Jesus was, the answer Jesus gave him made him more confused:

> *"Jesus answered and said unto him, verily, verily, I say unto except a man be born again, he cannot see the kingdom of God".*
>
> **John 3:3**

This is the very core of the beginning of every believer's journey or walk with God. This is like initiation or betrothal to a bridegroom. Jesus simply meant in order to see the kingdom of God, the place we are trying to go or journey to, you must be born again. You must accept the owner of the kingdom by the baptism of water and the Spirit of God.

> *"He who believes and is baptized will be saved; but he who does not believe will be condemned".*
>
> **Mark 16:16**

Now Nicodemus' response: "Nicodemus said unto him, 'How can a man be born again when he is old? Can he enter the second time into his mother's womb and be born?'" (John 3:4). Nicodemus was thinking more physical than spiritual, something which most believers still do because it is hard to allow the Spirit to lead us. More often, we are interested in theology and what we can see. But in the kingdom of God, we don't operate by the principle of "seeing is believing," which is contrary to faith, but rather by "believing is seeing," which was the process of being saved also in the Old Testament.

> *"And Abraham believed, and the Lord and he counted it to him for righteousness".*
>
> **Genesis 15:6**

> *"Even as Abraham believed God, and it was accounted to him for righteousness".*
>
> **Galatians 3:6**

Jesus went straight into the state of Nicodemus' spiritual life by telling him he must be born again. Now this is a very important issue as statement because it allows everybody to be able to see and enter the kingdom of God without any exceptions.

> *"But as many as received him to them, he gave the right to become children of God to those who believed in his name who were born not of blood nor of the will of the flesh,*

nor of the will of man, but of God".

John 1:12-13

This means that you may have been born or entered this world through wedlock, rape, or born into a dead religion or Satanist and still become a part of God's family by believing in Jesus' name and accepting Him as your personal savior; all are very much welcome by our compassionate, loving God, hallelujah (no condemnation to those in God). This was and is still an open and ongoing invitation, even to you reading this book.

> "Behold, I stand at the door and knock. If anyone hears my voice and opens the door, I will come in to him and dine with him, and he with me".
>
> **Revelation 3:20**

Now Nicodemus, being confused and curious, in the same time allowed Jesus to dive more into spiritual matters rather than physical.

> "Jesus answered, 'Most assuredly, I say to you, unless one is born of water and the Spirit, he cannot enter the kingdom of God. That which is born of the flesh is flesh, and that which is born of the Spirit is spirit. Do not marvel that I said to you, "You must be born again." **The wind blows where it wishes, and you** hear the sound of it, but cannot tell where it comes from and where it goes.

THE MYSTERY OF BEING BORN AGAIN

> *So is everyone who is born of the Spirit.' Nicodemus answered and said to Him, 'How can these things be?'".*
>
> **John 3:5-9**

It is normal to sometimes be blown away or confused about the ways the Spirit of God moves because of the fact that we are human and our understanding is very limited as compared to God's. Even when the angel of the Lord Gabriel came to Mary and announce to her that she would have a baby who's name would be Jesus and who would be the savior of the world, Mary was confused because she was not married and was still a virgin, and so she gave the same answer Nicodemus gave: "How can this be?"

> *"Then Mary said to the angel, 'How can this be, since I [a]do not know a man?' And the angel answered and said to her,* ***'The Holy Spirit will come upon you, and the power of the Highest will overshadow you; therefore, also, that Holy One who is to be born will be called the Son of God. Now indeed, Elizabeth your relative has also conceived a son in her old age; and this is now the sixth month for her who was called barren. For with God nothing will be impossible.'*** *Then Mary said, 'Behold the maidservant of the Lord! Let it be to me according to your word.' And the angel departed from her".*
>
> **Luke 1:34-38**

What Jesus was getting Nicodemus to understand was that to be born again had nothing to do with the birth canal of a woman, which is the natural birth. Jesus was talking about spiritual birth, which must involve water, which is the word of God and the Spirit of God. In the Old Testament, water most times represented the Scriptures, which is the word of God.

> *"Husbands love your wives, even as Christ also love the church and gave Himself for it: that he might sanctify and cleans it with the washing of water by the word that he might present it to himself a glorious church, not having a spot or wrinkle or any such thing, but that it should be holy and without blemish".*
> **Ephesians 5:25-27**

Notice that both scriptures above speak of how the word of God is used to **cleanse** a man from his ways and from any blemishes. This is why we noticed that the thief on the cross next to Jesus on the day of crucifixion didn't go through water baptism but still made it to heaven as Jesus said to him clearly, "today you will be with me in paradise."

> *"Then one of the criminals who were hanged blasphemed Him, saying, 'If you are the Christ, save yourself and us.; But the other, answering, rebuked him, saying, 'Do you not even fear God, seeing you are under the same*

condemnation? And we indeed justly, for we receive the due reward of our deeds; but this Man has done nothing wrong.' **Then he said to Jesus,** *'Lord, remember me when you come into your kingdom.' And Jesus said to him, 'Assuredly, I say to you, today you will be with me in Paradise'".*

Luke 23:39-43

Also, let's take a look at another scripture below, which will throw more light on this subject matter:

"If we confess, our sins, He is faithful, and just to forgive us our sins and to cleanse us from all unrighteousness".

1 John 1:9

Physical water can only cleanse a man's physical body but cannot cleanse a man's soul from unrighteousness, which in other words is called wickedness. It is the word of God that changes the heart condition of a man from wickedness to holiness and righteousness. Just as the cross is a symbol of our salvation through grace and faith in Jesus Christ, water baptism can also be seen as a symbol to initiate us into our journey with Christ, but it's the word of God that actually does the work together with the Spirit of God. The word of God and the Spirit of God must be married and intertwine in us to be able to walk and stay in the spirit. So Nicodemus had and knew the word of God, taught it to others skillfully, but was lacking the Spirit of God to understand better and demonstrate power. So the Bible says, "in all thy getting, get understanding." Getting understanding is allowing the word and Spirit of God to come into you to teach you and is the best that can happen to any man. This is how the new birth takes place, and it's such an awesome experience. Jesus said in John 3:8, "the wind blows where it wishes, and you hear the sound of it, but cannot tell where it comes from and where it goes. So is everyone who is born of the Spirit."

Pneuma is the Greek word for both wind and Spirit. So Jesus was saying, no one can see the wind and which way it is blowing, only its effects. In the same way, no one can see the new birth happening, but the results of the Spirit's life-changing work are evident. The transformation becomes clear in a man who walks with God. There is a great story of Abraham finding a bride for his son, Isaac, by sending his oldest servant in Genesis 24. The Spirit of the Lord gave me great understanding into this passage to illustrate:

a) How to be born again.

b) How to see the kingdom of God, as it was Jesus' first answer to Nicodemus.

c) How to enter the kingdom of God, which was the second answer.

d) The mystery of the wind blowing, but no one knows where it's coming from.

e) Finally, the evidence of the life transforming work the wind (Spirit of God) does in a person.

Simple illustration of being born again seeing and entering the kingdom of God using Abraham story and Genesis 24.

This is by a great means to bring understanding to those who lack understanding about being born again, as many have argued and rejected or are already in the kingdom but lack understanding.

We will lay emphasis on some key scriptures in Genesis 24, but I suggest you read the whole chapter with the help of the Holy Spirit to get a clear picture of this great illustration. In this story here, I will represent the characters to the Trinity, God the Father, God the Son, and God the Holy Spirit, and other characters will represent souls or people in the Earth and salvation process.

> *"Abraham was old well advanced in age and the Lord had blessed Abraham in all things. So Abraham said to the oldest servant of his house who ruled over all that he had, 'Please put your hand under my thigh, and I will make you swear by the Lord, the God of heaven and God of the Earth that you will not take a wife for my son from the daughters of the Canaanites, among whom I dwell, but you shall go to my country and to my family and take a wife for my son Isaac'".*
>
> **Genesis 24:1-4**

In this passage, we will represent God's character with Abraham, who is sending his oldest servant in his house as the Holy Spirit to look for a bride as souls for his son Isaac, who is Jesus Christ. Remember after the death and resurrection and ascension of our Lord Jesus Christ, the Holy Spirit is the person moving in the world, touching, convicting, and drawing souls into the kingdom of God as the bride of Jesus. So Abraham sent his oldest servant to a distant land to search for this bride just as the Holy Spirit is using people today to win souls

> "...and the servant said to him, 'Perhaps the woman will not be willing to follow me to this land. Must I take your son back to the land from which you come?' But Abraham said to him, '...if the woman is not willing to follow you, then you will be released from this oath only do not take my son back there'".
> **Genesis 24:5-8**

As you have read, the servant was worried that the woman would not listen and follow him, something that happens as the Spirit of the Lord is accepted or welcome by some and rejected by others because they don't feel the connection or are simply rebellious. The Bible says in John 14:17 that the Spirit of truth the world cannot receive, because it neither sees Him nor knows Him, but you know Him, for He dwells with you and will be in you. So as per the scripture, the servant was instructed by the master to go to his country or kindred for the bride for his son. In his country, there is a connection between them. Abraham knew that his servant could find a good wife for his son Isaac. Just as the Bible says in Romans 8:29-31, "For whom He did foreknow, He also did predestinate to be conformed to the image of His Son, that he might be the first born among many brethren. Moreover whom he did predestinate, them He also called: and whom He called, them He also justified: and whom He justified, them He also glorified. What shall we then say to these things? If God be for us, who can be against us?"

This means as long as the bride feels the connection and is willing to go with the servant to Abraham to be the bride of Isaac, she will be accepted, and no one can say no to Abraham, and she will be glorified as Abraham was rich, and no one could be against her.

> "No man can come to me, except the Father which has sent me draw him, and I will raise him up at the last day".
> **John 6:44**

With the above scripture and storyline, no one could go to Isaac, unless Abraham bought them through the servant; so it is that it is the Spirit of God draws men to Jesus and not ourselves, and it is God who chooses us and not ourselves. It is God who finds us and not us who finds God. Genesis 24:12-21 shows how the servant of Abraham found the soon-to-be-wife of Isaac at the well. Then he said, "'O Lord God of my master Abraham, please give me success this day, and show kindness to my master Abraham. Behold, *here* I stand by the well of water, and the daughters of the men of the city are coming out to draw water. Now let it be that the young woman to whom I say, "Please let down your pitcher that I may drink," and she says, "Drink, and I will also give your camels a drink"—*let* her *be the one* You have appointed for Your servant Isaac. And by this I will know that You have shown kindness to my master.' And it happened, before he had finished speaking, that behold, Rebekah, who was born to Bethuel, son of Milcah, the wife of Nahor, Abraham's brother, came out with her pitcher on her shoulder. Now the young woman *was* very beautiful to behold, a virgin; no man had known her. And she went down to the well, filled her pitcher, and came up. And the servant ran to meet her and said, 'Please let me drink a little water from your pitcher.' So she said, 'Drink, my lord.' Then she quickly let her pitcher down to her hand and gave him a drink. And when she had finished giving him a drink, she said, 'I will draw *water* for your camels also, until they have finished drinking.' Then she quickly emptied her pitcher into the trough, ran back to the well to draw *water,* and drew for all his camels. And the man, wondering at her, remained silent so as to know whether the Lord had made his journey prosperous or not" (Genesis 24:12-21).

Rebecca unknowingly comes to the well to fetch water for the servant to drink and give some to the camels to drink as well, which the servant was using as a confirmation for Isaac's bride. The Holy Spirit uses various means to encounter and draw individuals to be the bride of Jesus Christ, the only son of God. Some encounter Him in their low moment, through a friend, movies, dreams, church services, conferences, or evangelism, hallelujah. I believe you are now remembering your first encounter with the Holy Spirit and how beautiful it was.

Please share your story on our pages and website and let the world know so others can be drawn as well (Kindly add the links etc.).

So Rebekah, coming to the well on a regular day to perform her assignment, didn't know that Abraham had predestined or instructed for a wife to be brought from her country, which was Abraham and Isaac's country as well, and Rebecca shared a blood relation with Abraham. You are not a coincidence or an accident in the Kingdom of God; you were predestined, chosen and cherished, hallelujah. You can never think for a second that you are a mistake in the Kingdom of God. The Holy Spirit touching you was a strategic plan of God to bring you back into His Kingdom to reveal your purpose, change your life, and cause you to walk with kings and queens since you are God's prized asset and His son loves you so much to die for you. The scripture says in John 15:16, "You did not choose me, but I chose you and appointed you so that you might go and bear fruit that will last and so that whatever you ask in my name, the father will give you." Glory to God! Rebecca was going to take care of her day-to-day business and didn't know that there was such a great seed fruit in her womb waiting to be birthed and that that seed would last forever. A whole nation in the form of Jacob and Esau was inside of her, as we are all descendants of Jacob who became Israel.

> *"And God said to him, 'Your name is **Jacob; your name shall not be called Jacob anymore, but Israel shall be your name.**' So He called his name Israel".*
> **Genesis 35:10**

It took a divine encounter to the father's (Abraham) servant to connect her to Isaac, and now we are all a generation from this encounter and seed. You are not a failure, and God did not create garbage, so the day you heard the gospel or as you read this book, know that it is an appointed time set aside for you to be separated unto Abba for exploits

> *"But you are a chosen generation, a royal priesthood, a holy nation, his own special people that you may proclaim the praises of Him who called you out of darkness into his marvelous light, who once were not a people now the people of God who had not obtained mercy, but now I have obtained mercy".*
> **1 Peter 2:9-10**

Just as Rebecca was special, just as the Spirit of the Lord led the servant to encounter her, you are peculiar in this kingdom and your assignment and blessings are for you and nobody else.

> *"And it came to pass, when Abraham's servant heard their words, that he worshiped the Lord, bowing himself to the earth. Then the servant brought out jewelry of silver, jewelry of gold, and clothing, and gave them to Rebekah. He also gave precious things to her brother and to her mother. And he and the men who were with him ate and drank and stayed all night. Then they arose in the morning, and he said, 'Send me away to my master.' But her brother and her mother said, 'Let the young woman stay with us a few days, at least ten; after that she may go.' And he said to them, 'Do not hinder me, since the Lord has prospered my way; send me away so that I may go to my master.' So they said, 'We will call the young woman and ask her personally.' Then they called Rebekah and said to her, 'Will you go with this man?' And she said, 'I will go.'"*
>
> **Genesis 24:52-58**

First, we noticed that, just by Rebecca accepting the proposal, she is decorated with the Royal ornaments, which Abraham's servant brought along, and even some of the blessings are given to the family members. This right here shows that as you make yourself available at the feet of Jesus as His bride, you are not the only beneficiary of his Father's blessings, but your family and household are all able to enter into the supernatural grace and provision of

God, our Father. Scriptures say that because of Cornelius, the entire household was saved as he was led by the angel to call for Peter to come and preach the gospel of Jesus Christ.

> "Then Peter opened his mouth and said: 'In truth I perceive that God shows no partiality. But in every nation whoever fears Him and works righteousness is accepted by Him. The word which God sent to the children of Israel, preaching peace through Jesus Christ—He is Lord of all— that word you know, which was proclaimed throughout all Judea, and began from Galilee after the baptism which John preached: how God anointed Jesus of Nazareth with the Holy Spirit and with power, who went about doing good and healing all who were oppressed by the devil, for God was with Him. And we are witnesses of all things which He did both in the land of the Jews and in Jerusalem, whom they killed by hanging on a tree. Him God raised up on the third day, and showed Him openly, not to all the people, but to witnesses chosen before by God, even to us who ate and drank with Him after He arose from the dead. And He commanded us to preach to the people, and to testify that it is He who was ordained by God to be Judge of the living and the dead. To Him all the prophets

witness that, through His name, whoever believes in Him will receive remission of sins.' While Peter was still speaking these words, the Holy Spirit fell upon all those who heard the word. And those of the circumcision who believed were astonished, as many as came with Peter, because the gift of the Holy Spirit had been poured out on the Gentiles also. For they heard them speak with tongues and magnify God. Then Peter answered, 'Can anyone forbid water, that these should not be baptized who have received the Holy Spirit just as we have?' And he commanded them to be baptized in the name of the Lord. Then they asked him to stay a few days".

Acts 10:34-48

We can mention some few names who, because of their acceptance and availability, saved a whole generation and household, like **Noah, Rehab, Ruth, Esther, Lydia, the Apostles** to mention a few. I believe it is your turn now to do exploits, to be God's channel of blessing to your family, community, nation, and the world. Let me quickly point it out to you by the lead of the Holy Spirit that, in Genesis 24:55, I noticed that the brother and sister wanted to be a distraction by delaying Rebekah and the servant from traveling immediately to join Abraham and Isaac the bridegroom. This is exactly what happens to most of us when we encounter the Spirit of the Lord at a Kairos moment; we let families, careers, plans, desires, positions, etc. distract and delay us from accepting our divine calling and mandate.

> *"But her brother and her mother said, 'Let the young woman stay with us a few days, at least ten; after that she may go'".*
>
> **Genesis 24:55**

It brings us back to how Nicodemus who knew the Bible and was a great teacher was hindered by his position in society to freely follow Jesus immediately, whilst the woman at the well who was from Samaria, did not know much, left everything immediately to evangelize and follow Jesus. What a striking difference between these two important figures in the Bible.

PRAYER

Dear Jesus, I know I am a sinner and I have sinned against you. Please forgive me and cleanse me with your blood that you shared on the calvary cross. I accept you today as my personal savior; come into my life and baptize me with your Spirit, amen.

And if you are already a born-again Christian but feel like you have not given your best to Jesus, or fell back, please pray this prayer with me:

PRAYER

Dear Lord, please help me by your Spirit and grace to restore unto me the Joy of my Salvation. I want to burn for you again and be a living sacrifice and a channel through which other people can know you and be saved, in Jesus mighty name, amen.

N/B: Please find a good church home to connect and fellowship with the brethren so you can be strengthened and sharpened daily as the Bible says in Hebrews 10:25, "not forsaking the assembling of ourselves together, as *is* **the manner of some, but exhorting** *one another,* **and so much the more** as you see the Day approaching."

CHAPTER FIVE

BUILDING A STRONG, FUNCTIONAL RELATIONSHIP

"Every functioning relationship is a product of investment of time and efforts!"

    We have seen in previous chapters what it takes to build a great relationship and what's required of an individual. The word "functional" is defined in the Oxford dictionary as something designed to be practical and useful rather than attractive. This means that this relationship you are building with Christ must be practical, useful, and must produce a great desired result and fruits that will be beneficial not only to you but to your family and friends, as it happened in the house of Cornelius when Peter went to preach to his people. This chapter is to help you initiate a relationship with Christ or better your relationship with Him, depending on where you stand with Christ. You may not have a relationship at all like Rehab who was considered a prostitute, but one great faith move got her and her household saved. You may be in the position of the Samarian woman at the well when she encountered Jesus; she had heard of Him but didn't know who He was and how to serve and worship Him. You may be like Ruth, following Naomi blindly, but ending up serving Naomi and her God and becoming a great grandmother of the Messiah. You may be in the position of Saul who was persecuting the church because he lacked understanding that the church is Christ, and his life change when he encountered Jesus, and his name change from Saul to Paul, and he became one of the greatest apostles of Jesus. You may be in a position of Peter, who was minding his business and fishing as his career and didn't know the great calling he had but encountered Jesus and became the rock upon which Christ built the church.

Wherever you are in this journey of life, it is my desire to help you encounter Jesus through understanding and stir up your spirit to begin walking in your purpose and fulfilling your God-given mandate here on earth. Remember this: The Lord is already proud of you, and you will be very great! It will be wise to say, do not enter into any relationship with an ulterior motive, especially with your mind focused on only what you can get; many people end up disappointed in relationships that could have ended well and beautiful; because the fact that their heart condition was not right, it ended up in fights disagreements, separation, divorce, anger, jealousy, and pain. As an apostle of God pastoring the Lord's flock, I can tell you how many people are bitter and angry at Jesus because they feel disappointed that the reason why they came to Him has not been fulfilled. Sometimes as people are evangelizing or trying to win souls for the kingdom, they innocently or unconsciously because of zeal make promises of materialism, and people come to the kingdom with the heart full of materialism and vanity.

> *"Jesus answered them and said, 'Most assuredly, I say to you, you seek Me, not because you saw the signs, but because you ate of the loaves and were filled'".*
>
> **John 6:26**

How many people today are in church for financial breakthrough, for a miracle of healing, business growth, or for marriage, etc. and it is not wrong, but your priority must first be knowing Jesus and loving Him with all of you.

> *"For after all these things the Gentiles seek. For your heavenly Father knows that you need all these things. But seek first the kingdom of God and His righteousness, and all these things shall be added to you".*
>
> **Matthew 6:32-33**

Our father in heaven knows all our desires, burdens, pain, lack, sicknesses, and all that we are crying about, but He also most importantly desires a genuine, father-son/

daughter relationship with us, filled with love, compassion, joy, happiness, and fulfillment. Again, I have seen many people, countless people, run to church in tears, seeking miracles and solutions to a problem after they have tried everything in the book and out of the book—I mean, even other gods and dark practices—and when it didn't work for them, they came to church, got the miracle or the solution to that problem and never came back again. They didn't leave me, but rather they left Christ and the kingdom.

TESTIMONY

I prayed with someone before for the release of their money which was denied for years, and when it was released, he left and never came back. He began indulging in dark activities with the money and was later found dead. In this case, the miracle killed him because he could not control the big sum of money that came to him. He was not matured enough in Christ to continue on the narrow path with all that money. That is not the intention that God has for His children, but He first wants to mature them, then bless them and bring them to an expected end.

> *"For I know the thoughts that I think toward you, says the Lord, thoughts of peace and not of evil, to give you a future and a hope".*
> **Jeremiah 29:11**

In chapter 6, we saw how Rebecca who had never seen Isaac before didn't know if he was good-looking, rich, or poor, but went with a genuine intention to love him and be his wife, and the marriage was glorious and produced great seed. This is the kind of mindset we need to come to Christ with, to love Him, be with Him, make His vision our vision, our burdens, and everything He has will automatically be ours; we will be His bride, and the bride is a joint owner of whatever the bridegroom owns as we read and the story of Esther who was told by the king to ask for half of the kingdom, and it would be hers.

> *"And the king said to her, 'What do you wish, Queen Esther? What is your request? It shall be given to you—up to half the kingdom!'"*.
>
> **Esther 5:3**

> *"And when Herodias' daughter herself came in and danced, and pleased Herod and those who sat with him, the king said to the girl, 'Ask me whatever you want, and I will give it to you.' He also swore to her, 'Whatever you ask me, I will give you, up to half my kingdom.' So she went out and said to her mother, 'What shall I ask?' And she said, 'The head of John the Baptist!' Immediately she came in with haste to the king and asked, saying, 'I want you to give me at once the head of John the Baptist on a platter.' And the king was exceedingly sorry; yet, because of the oaths*

> *and because of those who sat with him, he did not want to refuse her. Immediately the king sent an executioner and commanded his head to be brought. And he went and beheaded him in prison, brought his head on a platter, and gave it to the girl; and the girl gave it to her mother".*
>
> **Mark 6:22-28**

The revelation here is that even ordinary men for the sake of their position, prestige, credibility, integrity, and honor, fulfilled their vow, even when it hurt their emotions and went against the principles and made them exceedingly sorry; yet they did it immediately. So you can imagine the k=King of kings and the Lord of the lords, whose word or promises are more credible than the words of any man.

> *"God is not a man, that He should lie, Nor a son of man, that He should repent. Has He said, and will He not do? Or has He spoken, and will He not make it good?"*
>
> **Numbers 23:19**

We serve a God who does not change His mind nor lie, so when He says, seek Him first and His kingdom and righteousness and everything else will be added to it, then He knows and means what He is saying and has the capacity and capability to make it happen. He does not go back on His word and will not take your faith in Him for granted at all; His name, integrity, and credibility are on the line here, as well. Remember the Israelites, even when they were stiff necked, disobedient, and disloyal, He said to Moses to step aside for Him to kill them and raise Moses a new people, and Moses said, if He did that, the nations would say He brought them out of Egypt but could not fulfill His promise, and God relented and took them to the promised land. His name and word are everything to him.

> *"For all the promises of God in Him are Yes, and in Him Amen, to the glory of God through us".*
>
> **2 Corinthians 1:20**

David said in Psalms 138:2, "I will worship toward Your holy temple, And praise Your name For Your lovingkindness and Your truth; For You have magnified Your word above all Your name."

His word is His word, and he fulfills it to the end.

> *"For as the rain comes down, and the snow from heaven, and do not return there, But water the earth, and make it bring forth and bud, that it may give seed to the sower and bread to the eater, So shall My word be that goes forth from My mouth; It shall not return to Me void, But it shall accomplish what I please, And it shall prosper in the thing for which I sent it".*
>
> **Isaiah 55:10-11**

Hallelujah! So when the Lord says, serve me and I will bless you, you are very much secured in this promise, and nothing can stop him from fulfilling that promise. I am going to give you a few scriptures that will stir up your faith and will show you the four steps to follow to build your functional relationship with the Son of the King.

> *"You shall not bow down to their gods, nor serve them, nor do according to their works; but you shall utterly overthrow them and completely break down their sacred pillars. So you shall serve the Lord your God, and He will bless your bread and your water. And I will take sickness away from the midst of you. No one shall suffer miscarriage or be barren in your land; I will fulfill the number of your days. I will send My fear before you, I will cause confusion among all the people to whom you come, and will make all your enemies turn their backs to you".*
> **Exodus 23:24-26**

a) He is a jealous God and wants your full attention and for you to serve Him without being lukewarm.

b) Don't follow the worldly practices and religious activities, which look good in the eye but are very empty and vain.

c) We live in the days where all our food and water are no longer clean, but He will protect you from it.

The Bible says in Mark 16:18, "They[a] will take up serpents; and if they drink anything deadly, it will by no means hurt them; they will lay hands on the sick, and they will recover." In Acts 28:3-6, when Paul had gathered a bundle of sticks and laid them on the fire, a viper came out because of the heat, and fastened on his hand. So when the natives saw the creature hanging from his hand, they said to one another, "No doubt this man is a murderer, whom, though he has escaped the sea, yet justice does not allow to live." But he shook off the creature into the fire and suffered no harm. However, they were expecting that he would swell up or suddenly fall down dead. But after they had looked for a long time and saw no harm come to him, they changed their minds and said that he was a god. The true presence of God in your life brings supernatural protection, which blows minds. The evil can happen, but it cannot kill you, and on-lookers and enemies will always testify that you serve a living God.

    d) He will take sickness away from you

    e) No one shall suffer miscarriage. Let me explain this well for you: Miscarriage is when a conceived baby comes out prematurely but business ideas, marriages, life plans, etc. can be miscarried also and come out prematurely and collapse, so this means whatever good and great thing you carry will mature well and come out at the right time as a great seed, and you will bear great fruits, and your ideas, plans, marriage, etc. will not die early. You will not suffer losses.

f) Your land will not be baron means whatever you plant a seed, a business, an idea, or start something, it will come out great; you will be fruitful. You will not suffer emptiness but rather experience abundance.

g) He will make sure you will live life to the fullest and not die a foolish death or prematurely.

h) Finally, you know, success breeds enemies for no reason, so he will protect you and cause your enemies to look away and not even fight you

THE FIVE STEPS IN BUILDING YOUR RELATIONSHIP

a) Studying the word of God.

b) Prayer/meditation.

c) Worship

d) Services unto the Lord

e) Spiritual Guidance through a Mentor

We are going to take each step one-by-one and see how we can incorporate it into our daily lives to build a beautiful functional relationship with Christ.

STUDYING THE WORD OF GOD.

Let's first begin by defining the word of God. Scripture defines the word of God as a person who is Jesus Christ:

"In the beginning was the Word, and the Word was with God, and the Word was God. He was in the beginning with God. All things were made through Him, and without Him nothing was made that was made. In Him was life, and the life was the light of men. And the light shines in the darkness, and the darkness did not comprehend it" (John 1:1-5). The Word of God is also the divine revelation of God breathed out by the Spirit of God, which is the creative force and flow of God. It is the absolute truth spoken by God through holy men under the inspiration of the Holy Spirit. To break down the above scripture to bring clear understanding, we will take it step-by-step to see why it is very important to study the Word of God.

- "In the beginning was the Word": This means that before creation, He existed, and he was not created.

- "And the Word was with God": He was with the God head, that's the Father.

- "And the Word was God": This settles the debate of whether Jesus is God or not.

- "All things were made by Him": Whatever you see in nature, its beauty and splendor, was made by Jesus who desires a relationship with his fallen creation to restore them back.

- "Without Him was not anything made that was made": There was nothing that was made without Jesus.

He is the creative power of God, so this means that in studying the word of God, you are actually studying Jesus; it is like studying your partner or spouse to know them better and understand them to be able to make them happy. Also, since He is the creative force of God, it means in studying the Word you are actually studying to be creative as in obtaining power for signs and wonders. **"Remember you become whatever you study" (Apostle Jeremiah).** If you study medicine, you become a doctor. If you study cooking, you become a chef. If you study electricity and current, you become an electrician. If you study the Creator Jesus, you become creative; at least, you can be inspired by the Holy Spirit with an idea to create things that will help humanity and bring you financial blessings and connections. Many great inventors back then were all followers of Christ, like the Wright brothers who invented an airplane and Thomas Edison who invented the lightbulb. They will tell you how they had a dream or revelation as they slept and woke up to begin researching and working it out. Your time has come, too. Hallelujah.

- In Him was life. Remember, after creating man, He breathed into him before he became a living soul, so when you move away from the source of life, you start dying, but when you study the life-giving force and stay close, you will live to fulfill the number of your days.
- The life of Jesus is the light of men. **"And this is the condemnation, that the light has come**

into the world, and men loved darkness rather than light, because their deeds were evil" (John 3:19).

In order for your light as a man to shine, you must stay closer to the source of light so you can reflect more. The closer you are, the brighter you will be and the more glorious your life will be with favor, grace, and mercies going ahead of you and all of your endeavors to bring you victories. David said in Psalm 119:105, "Your word *is* a lamp to my feet And a light to my path."

- Finally, the light shineth in darkness, and the darkness comprehended it not.

No matter how dark a room is, even when you are a light as small as a candle or flashlight, you will see the differences, and its illumination can help you navigate your way in the room. Absence of the light in a place can cause men to keep stumbling until they are injured and can't move again. That is why the moment the power goes off in the house, the first thing everybody looks for is the flashlight and not their money; light leads you to your money and everything else in the house. But unfortunately, we want to put aside the light and look for money and miracles first, and that is why men in our generation are not effective. When you are the only one in a dark room with a flashlight, everybody will run to you because they want to see, walk, and not stumble; so wherever you go, they will follow you, and that will make you a leader and not a follower.

Also, as Jesus walked, the forces of darkness bowed to Him because He was light; that is why you need light, so evil will flee from you in these dark ages. The fallen angels were all light bearers until they rebelled, and God casted they out of His presence, and they became dark. In Hebrews 4:12, the Bible says, "For the word of God *is* living and powerful, and sharper than any two-edged sword, piercing even to the division of soul and spirit, and of joints and marrow, and is a discerner of the thoughts and intents of the heart."

The word of God is truly living and active because it has the ability to bring change and transformation to your life. It is sharper than any two edged sword. Remember, a soldier always needs a sword to attack the enemies or opposition. As a child of God, the only way you can be on offensive in spiritual warfare is by having the word of God, which is the sword of the Spirit as **Ephesians 6:17 says when apostle Paul was teaching on spiritual warfare: "And take the helmet of salvation, and the sword of the Spirit, which is the word of God**." Many Christians are under attack today; when I say under attack, I mean in the defensive mode against the enemies because they don't have enough word in them to combat the enemy. Sickness, diseases, broken homes, sudden deaths are on the rise because many are in churches today seeking only prophecies and not to be students of the word. If you are always on the defense mode, the chances of the enemy striking you are higher, but when you have enough word and are always on the attack, then the enemy backs off from you and you put him on the back foot. There are also two types of the word of God:

- Logos is the written word in the Bible that we study.

- Rhema is the Holy Ghost inspired word that comes to you during prayers or declarations, especially when you are deep in the Spirit, that usually brings the answers or solutions to a particular problem you are dealing with.

It is the live and active word that stirs your spirit to make you know God has spoken to you concerning your issue or prayer request. The word of God also serves as a guide to us, and we should live an acceptable life as a child of God. 2 Timothy 3:16-17 says, "All Scripture *is* given by inspiration of God, and *is* profitable for doctrine, for reproof, for correction, for instruction in righteousness, that the man of God may be complete, thoroughly equipped for every good work."

> *"It is the Spirit who gives life; the flesh profits nothing. The words that I speak to you are spirit, and they are life".*
> **John 6:63**

These were the very words of Jesus, that the words he speaks have the ability to spring forth life in men because they are spirit and are a life-giving force. After we become born again, we had to go through a sanctification process to be able to walk in purity and holiness, and it is actually the word of God that has the ability to do this, as the Bible says in John 17:17: "Sanctify them by Your truth. Your word is truth." As children of God, we are commanded to walk in faith and not by sight, and in order to build your faith, you must constantly hear and be in touch with the word of God.

> *"So then faith comes by hearing, and hearing by the word of God".*
> **Romans 10:17**

Your faith can actually die or be very low when you are not studying and hearing the word of God. Jesus said to the disciples in Matthew 13:11, **"Because it has been given to you to know the mysteries of the kingdom of heaven, but to them it has not been given."** Glory belongs to God who has not hidden his mysteries but revealed them to us through his Word. It is the mysteries that bring healing, deliverance, restoration, miracles, signs, and wonders. In conclusion, for you to be blessed, you must desire to hear the word and keep it, meaning obey it. Luke 11:28 says, "More than that, blessed are those who hear the word of God and keep it!"

In Joshua 1:8, God gave young Joshua a charge that will make him great after succeeding his spiritual-giant master Moses, and He said, **"This Book of the Law shall not depart from your mouth, but you[a] shall meditate in it day and night, that you may observe to do according to all that is written in it. For then you will make your way prosperous, and then you will have good success."**

So in order to prosper and have good success (notice that there is success and good success), you must study and obey the word of God. Good success is what I call sustainable success. Some successes are seasonal and cut off and leave you empty or destroyed, so knowing your word helps you build great confidence in prayers because you know you are asking according to His will, which generates results. The confidence also comes because you know He hears you, and if He hears you, He will surely answer you; that is, when you leave your prayer room smiling and when you begin seeing answers, you will begin to love praying.

I always tell people, results are very addictive, more than drugs. Those who often times don't get results ask amiss because, even though they are asking, they are doing so not in accordance with the will of God but to satisfy the lust of their flesh. "You ask and do not receive, because you ask amiss, that you may spend *it* on your pleasures" (James 4:3). May you desire for the word of God to increase greatly, and may he give you understanding as you begin a new adventure of studying the word.

PRAYER/MEDITATION

Moving to the next step, which is prayer and meditation, I would like to point out to you that it is actually the Word of God that enables you to pray and pray effectively because it starts your spirit and faith up and enables you to talk to God in the spirit and not in your flesh.

> *"Now this is the confidence that we have in Him, that if we ask anything according to His will, He hears us. ^{15} And if we know that He hears us, whatever we ask, we know that we have the petitions that we have asked of Him".*
>
> **1 John 5:14-15**

Prayer is simply communication between humans and our God, the means through which we talk to God. When we pray, we commune with our Creator, and we are able to thank, praise, worship, and also bring our supplications before Him. It is a moment where we really get intimate with Him; without communication there's no relationship even on the human level; no marriage, friendship, or relationship will survive without communication. On the other hand, a good healthy and strong communication also creates a great atmosphere for every relationship to thrive in. Through communication, you get to know what your partner or spouse likes and what makes them happy, and you are able to make adjustments based on their needs. You are also able to let your partner know how you feel and vice versa. Lack of communication has destroyed a lot of friendships, relationships, marriages, and homes, so there is a need for day-to-day communication to create a strong bond between two people. Now the Bible says in **John 4:24, "God *is* Spirit, and those who worship Him must worship in spirit and truth."** This means when talking to God, He will not be sitting in front of you physically like humans do, and this is why most Christians are not able to spend quality time with Him. We are so used to speaking directly to people and hearing them talking back right away with an audible voice, sign, or body language. This is why we must exercise patience, determination, and perseverance, in order to build our prayer life. The more consistent you are in prayer, the more real God will become to you and even the greater and clearer you will hear Him in prayer, talking back to you, and you will begin to feel closer and start enjoying prayer. Always remember that consistency is needed to build a great momentum and a strong prayer life, and everybody can do it, including you. Once you start seeing results, you will get addicted to the voice of God and excited about answered prayers.

In **Matthew 6:9-13 Jesus was teaching the disciples how to pray: In this manner, therefore, pray:**

"Our Father in heaven,
Hallowed be Your name.
Your kingdom come.
Your will be done
On earth as *it is* in heaven.
Give us this day our daily bread.
And forgive us our debts,
As we forgive our debtors.
And do not lead us into temptation,
But deliver us from the evil one.
For Yours is the kingdom and the power and the glory forever. Amen."

So based on this prayer, we can draw five good essentials from it.

- **Praise/adoration and Thanksgiving.**
- **Submission to the Father's will.**
- **Petition.**
- **Confession.**
- **Intercession**

As you are led by the Spirit of the Lord and these essentials, you can begin building a beautiful, effective, and functional prayer life. Jesus made a profound statement and **Matthew 6:5;** when he was speaking about prayer to the disciples, he said, "And when you pray, you shall not be like the hypocrites. For they love to pray standing in the synagogues and on the corners of the streets, that they may be seen by men. Assuredly, I say to you, they have their reward." The focus here is "**when you pray**"; notice that he did not say "**if you pray.**" The "when" means that you must and that prayer is an essential part of your life. Apostle Paul encourages us in 1 Thessalonians 5:17:18, "Pray without ceasing, in everything give thanks; for this is the will of God in Christ Jesus for you." You may ask, how one can pray continually? The more you continue to build momentum, you will begin to enjoy it so much. You will find yourself even praying when driving, at work, in the park, and almost everywhere; even when talking to people, your heart will still be in touch with the Spirit of God, and there will be prayers going on.

Prayer was the key element of Jesus ministry when he walked this earth, and that's how He prepared on a daily basis. Jesus prayed more than he preached or faced the crowd. Before Jesus made important decisions in his ministry, He engaged God in prayers for very long hours, and this is how He avoided errors in His ministry and earthly life.

> *"Now it came to pass in those days that He went out to the mountain to pray, and continued all night in prayer to God. And when it was day, He called His disciples to Himself; and from them He chose twelve whom He also named apostles".*
>
> **Luke 6:12-13**

Imagine you seeking the face of God in intense prayers before making major decisions like promoting people in your life and ministry, choosing who to marry, career, business ideas, and partners to work with; how impactful and insightful you will be to make those decisions! People are in trouble because they married wrong partners, promoted wrong people in their business, and the business shut down and made great losses, etc. Now, you might ask, but despite all those prayers, Judas was also chosen by Jesus and later betrayed Him, and the answer is, it was to fulfill scriptures, and Jesus clearly knew it right from the beginning, so He said to his disciples, when Peter said they have nowhere to go or they cannot follow anyone else, that

He chose the twelve himself, yet one of them would betray Him.

> *"But Simon Peter answered Him, 'Lord, to whom shall we go? You have the words of eternal life. Also we have come to believe and know that You are the Christ, the Son of the living God.' Jesus answered them, 'Did I not choose you, the twelve, and one of you is a devil?' He spoke of Judas Iscariot, the son of Simon, for it was he who would betray Him, being one of the twelve".*
>
> **John 6:68-71**

Another profound statement Jesus made was John 5:19 when they try to attack Him because of His works and calling God His own father. Then Jesus answered and said to them, "Most assuredly, I say to you, the Son can do nothing of Himself, but what He sees the Father do; for whatever He does, the Son also does in like manner." In order to know what someone who is away from you is doing, you must have some form of contact, and this was done through prayers. Prayer enables us to align our will to the will of God and builds our spirits for supernatural encounters in our lives. It facilitates good worship because you cannot worship effectively what you don't know, as Jesus told the Samaritan woman at the well. Worshiping someone you don't know takes you away from freedom to slavery and from grace back to being under the law.

> *"You worship what you do not know; we know what we worship, for salvation is of the Jews".*
>
> **John 4:22**

This was before through grace the gospel was preached to the Gentile, so now the window is opened for everybody to get to know our Almighty God through prayers

MEDITATION

Meditation is to focus your mind, heart, soul, and spirit on a particular subject, issue, message, plan, or some important action or decision you are about to make. In Christianity, meditation is the art of spending quality time with our God, being conscious of His presence around us, keeping our minds focused on His word in order to hear His voice to help us align to His will by surrendering our perspectives, time, and desires to Him. It is very important to practice meditation very often, especially after prayers because it opens up your spirit man for the Holy Spirit to talk back to you. Most people engage God in prayers; they pray and pray, and as soon as they are done, they leave and go mind their business. So it is like going to your bosses or parents to speak to them, and once you are done talking, you don't allow them the opportunity to speak back, and you leave. Imagine if you spoke to them concerning an issue that you are facing, and they don't get a chance to respond or advise you; you will still leave with the same issue because you left before receiving what you came for. The Bible even says it is more important to listen than to speak. So the problem with the majority of people these days is that they are speaking more than they are listening, and they are having more issues than solutions. Everybody has some deposit of wisdom in them, so we must practice listening to gain more from people when we meet them.

> *"So then, my beloved brethren, let every man be swift to hear, slow to speak, slow to wrath".*
> **James 1:19**

True listening demonstrates respect, builds trust, shows other people that you value their opinion, and it promotes deeper mutual understanding. Even when we went to pray, listening most times is not the first thing that comes to mine, but prayer is communion with God, who all wisdom, knowledge, council, and understanding is hidden in, so it is more important to spend time listening to what's on God's heart in addition to expressing what we also think and feel or desire. Most of the successful people I have known are the ones who do more listening than talking.

> *"Even a fool is counted wise when he holds his peace; When he shuts his lips, he is considered perceptive".*
> **Proverbs 17:28**

"A fool has no delight in understanding, but in expressing his own heart" (Proverbs 18:2). Always remember that the mind, opinion, and voice of instructions or directions are far more superior to your own opinion and plans. Men of the old knew how to meditate a lot, and they always heard from God and made the right moves. They didn't just move with the wave or follow the masses or new trends.

> *"And Isaac went out to meditate in the field in the evening; and he lifted his eyes and looked, and there, the camels were coming".*
> **Genesis 24:63**

This was when Isaac first set his eyes on Rebecca, his wife-to-be. What a moment to meet the woman you are about to marry, right before being in touch with God through meditation; you will not make error with that; it will not be about looks but discerning the spirit and heart of the woman to know if she is right for you and vice versa. David also said in **Psalm 1:2, "But his delight *is* in the law of the Lord, And in His law he meditates day and night."** Also in **Psalm 119:15, "I will meditate on Your precepts, And contemplate Your ways."** Meditation brings clarity, and it makes obedience easy as we see in the verses above. **"Make me understand the way of your precepts so shall I meditate on your wonderful works" (Psalm 119:27).** **"Now in the morning, having risen a long while before daylight, He went out and departed to a solitary place; and there He prayed" (Mark 1:35).** In the early hours of the morning, it is very quiet, and there are no distractions, and your spirit man and soul is quiet enough for you to focus. In moments like this, you get to hear from God and feel His presence.

No matter how busy your schedule is, without prayer and meditation you will be running on an empty tank and burn out. We also read about when Jesus fasted and prayed for forty days and forty nights in before encountering the tempter.

> *"Then Jesus was led up by the Spirit into the wilderness to be tempted by the devil. And when He had fasted forty days and forty nights, afterward He was hungry. Now when the tempter came to Him, he said, 'If You are the Son of God, command that these stones become bread.' But He answered and said, 'It is written, "Man shall not live by bread alone, but by every word that proceeds from the mouth of God."' Then the devil took Him up into the holy city, set Him on the pinnacle of the temple, and said to Him, 'If You are the Son of God, throw Yourself down. For it is written: "He shall give His angels charge over you," and, "In their hands they shall bear you up, Lest you dash your foot against a stone."' Jesus said to him, 'It is written again, "You shall not tempt the Lord your God."' Again, the devil took Him up on*

an exceedingly high mountain, and showed Him all the kingdoms of the world and their glory. And he said to Him, 'All these things I will give You if You will fall down and worship me.' Then Jesus said to him, [Away with you, Satan! For it is written, "You shall worship the Lord your God, and Him only you shall serve."' Then the devil left Him, and behold, angels came and ministered to Him".

Matthew 4:1-11

He overcame him because Jesus was so prepared spiritually during those periods of prayers and fasting. Prepare your spirit every day to be able to face life's battles and distractions to be great in life.

WORSHIP/SERVICES UNTO THE LORD

Worship is when we genuinely tell God how much we love Him through songs as we sing and praise Him, regardless of our situation or circumstances. It is also when we offer sacrifices, which is pleasing to the Lord to show our gratitude. There are many people in the Bible who offered worship and sacrifices that were rejected by God because of some factors

1. Their heart condition was not right
2. They did it grudgingly

3. They did not give their best
4. They did it for public display or to be seen
5. They did not take time to know who God really is

We see two brothers who engaged and sacrifice unto the Lord at the same time, but the little brother's sacrifice was accepted by the Lord; He rejected the older brother's sacrifice. This is to tell us that it is not about how long or what you know but the heart behind what you are giving.

> *"Then she bore again, this time his brother Abel. Now Abel was a keeper of sheep, but Cain was a tiller of the ground. And in the process of time it came to pass that Cain brought an offering of the fruit of the ground to the Lord. Abel also brought of the firstborn of his flock and of their fat. And the Lord respected Abel and his offering, but He did not respect Cain and his offering. And Cain was very angry, and his countenance fell. So the Lord said to Cain, 'Why are you angry? And why has your countenance fallen? If you do well, will you not be accepted? And if you do not do well, sin lies at the door. And its desire is for you, but you should rule over it.' [8] Now Cain talked with Abel his brother; and it came to pass, when they were in the field, that Cain rose up against Abel his brother and killed him".*
>
> **Genesis 4:2-8**

We see clearly in this passage that, even after his unrighteous sacrifice was rejected, he did not attempt to offer a better one but instead got rid of his brother, as if getting rid of his brother would automatically qualify him or get him accepted by the Lord as he would be the only choice. We see this pattern repeated in churches today by members in our family, workplaces, etc.. Most times when we have the privilege to do something, we do it anyhow, especially when we believe no one else can or is around to do it, until another person comes and does it right. That is when the wicked spirits like jealousy, envy, anger, backbiting, disappointment, gossip, etc. all begin to come into our spirit, and we start confusion and fight. We must always offer our best, even if we are alone or the only ones doing it. Serving the Lord is a privilege that we cannot take for granted at all. The Lord is just; when you do it right, He will be pleased. We must always keep in mind that whatever we do for the Lord must be done in faith, knowing that He sees and will surely reward us. So the scripture says and Hebrews 11:4, "By faith Abel offered to God a more excellent sacrifice than Cain, through which he obtained witness that he was righteous, God testifying of his gifts; and through it he being dead still speaks." They say your good deeds will always speak for you even in your absence.

"Bondservants, obey in all things your masters according to the flesh, not with eye-service, as men-pleasers, but in sincerity

of heart, fearing God. And whatever you do, do it heartily, as to the Lord and not to men, knowing that from the Lord you will receive the reward of the inheritance; for you serve the Lord Christ".

Colossians 3:22-24

PERSONAL TESTIMONY

I remember when I used to work as a delivery guy. I made sure I was always on time and very reliable, that the CEO of the business knew he could count on me even on my off days. Now, I was an individual contractor, meaning I could pick and choose when to work or basically reject jobs that I did not like. But I made myself available so much that whenever the company was in a jam, the CEO's first choice would be to tell the dispatches to call me, and I always said, "Yes, I am on it." Although he was not a believer and just a businessman, he looked at me one morning and said, "You are always dressed very clean like you are going to an office work, and you are a good representation of this business." I said thank you, and he said, "Wait. It's deeper than I just said." I asked him what he meant, and he said a lot of his customers put in requests for pickups and deliveries and said they wanted Driver number 87 or Prince, which was me, while rejecting other drivers. He said there were corporate buildings that he could only send me to because I was polite even when the customer had a delay. He proceeded to say something which came to pass, even though he was not a prophet; he looked at me and said, "If anybody will establish his own delivery company, it would be you." Shortly after, I was approached by clients to start my own business, and they signed contracts with me. They gave me the contracts without even having a business registration, and they had patience for me to register it. So I tell you, give your best in whatever you do, because you never know who is watching. Destiny helpers are always around, not only in church, silently watching our attitude and behaviors.

> *"And whatever you do in word or deed, do all in the name of the Lord Jesus, giving thanks to God the Father through Him".*
> **Colossians 3:17**

You must always bear in mind that, even outside of church, you have a ministry going on; your life is preaching the gospel more than your words. You are an ambassador of Christ, and when people hire you for work, business or in church, they must see a difference; when they listen to you, they must hear the wisdom of God, and that will make them want to follow you to serve your God. God doesn't want us to live a life full of hypocrisy where we act holy in church and evil in the house or workplace. If we refuse to give our best when we have the opportunity and privileged to do so, others will come later, offer their best, and our positions will be given to them without favoritism. Something happened one day in church service when Jesus walked the

Earth. He was in church service and witnessed firsthand an elderly lady gave her all quietly while rich people gave more but did it to be seen, and He acknowledged that the elderly woman indeed gave more than all of them.

> *"And He looked up and saw the rich putting their gifts into the treasury, and He saw also a certain poor widow putting in two mites. So He said, 'Truly I say to you that this poor widow has put in more than all; for all these out of their abundance have put in offerings for God, but she out of her poverty put in all the livelihood that she had'".*
> **Luke 21:1-4**

I always say to myself, no position is permanent, so I give my all wherever I go, so I will not be an easy disposable person. When I leave a place, they must feel my absence or the vacuum created by my absence through hard work, obedience, and excellence I displayed in my work. Then there is another art of worship which involves singing and praising the Lord with instruments for His grace and mercies.

> *"Let us come before His presence with thanksgiving; Let us shout joyfully to Him with psalms".*
> **Psalm 95:2**

We must always celebrate the goodness of the Lord with a grateful heart, which is able to create a charge of atmosphere for miracles to even happen to and for us. The Bible says when Paul and Silas were imprisoned, instead of complaining, which was going to be the easiest thing to do, they decided to sing hymns and pray, and an angel of the Lord appeared in the prison to break the chains and the gates and set them free.

> *"But at midnight Paul and Silas were praying and singing hymns to God, and the prisoners were listening to them. Suddenly there was a great earthquake, so that the foundations of the prison were shaken; and immediately all the doors were opened and everyone's chains were loosed".*
>
> **Acts 16:25-26**

These people were praying and worshiping because they trusted God and knew that their strength could do nothing in that situation they found themselves in, so they gave it up to God through worship, and God responded spectacularly. That is why in **Ephesians 5:19, the Bible says, "Speaking to one another in psalms and hymns and spiritual songs, singing and making melody in your heart to the Lord,"** it will be very easy to get together and complain about how difficult life is, but that won't bring solutions but, rather, more pain. The wisest thing to do is to edify each other through spiritual songs and praises unto God to enable Him to act on our behalf. The final and one of the most important sacrifices and worship is described by apostle Paul in Romans 12:1: "I beseech you therefore, brethren, by the mercies of God, that you present your bodies a living sacrifice, holy, acceptable to God, *which is* your reasonable service. This is set yourself apart as the living sacrifice, living a holy and righteous life and serving the Lord with all your heart."

When you give all of you to God, God gives you His all, and that is when the glory of God is poured out and you become a vessel of signs and wonders to your generation. It is a beautiful thing when you take time to know the Lord. As described in the opening pages of this chapter, it makes your worship and sacrifice easier because now you will be worshiping what you know. David said in **Psalms 69:30, "I will praise the name of God with a song, And will magnify Him with thanksgiving."** This is because he knows where his blessings, protection, and provision were coming from. So the next time you go to church, get involved and sing to God a new song and play skillfully with a shout of joy.

SPIRITUAL GUIDANCE THROUGH A MENTOR

This kind of spiritual mentoring is very powerfully self-transforming toward a functional relationship with Christ. In the perspective of Christian discipleship, a mentor is one ahead in their spiritual life who comes to offer wisdom, support, and encouragement toward a fellow believer in their journey with God. The process of mentoring is based on a very strong concept in Scripture that believers must develop their faith, overcome odds, and further develop their walk with Christ. One of the most famous instances of mentorship in the Bible has to be the relationship between Paul and Timothy. Already an experienced apostle, Paul took Timothy under his wing and schooled him on his spiritual journey. This mentor-mentee relationship, however, finds a beautiful expression in Paul's letters to Timothy composed of counsel, instruction, and encouragement. In 2 Timothy 1:13-14, Paul writes, "Follow the pattern of the sound words that you have heard from me, in the faith and love that are in Christ Jesus. By the Holy Spirit who dwells within us, guard the good deposit entrusted to you." In this passage, he further emphasizes to Timothy that sound teaching and faithfulness are to be followed, underlying the importance of holding fast to the truth learned and the dependence upon the Holy Spirit for guidance.

Mentorship has some significant benefits to anyone who would strongly desire to have a working relationship with Christ. The first and foremost is an accountability issue: It becomes so easy to slacken or turn away from the path of truth in our Christian walk. A mentor stands in as a way of keeping us answerable for the same, focused on attaining our spiritual goals, and living in accordance with the Word of God. Proverbs 27:17 states, "Iron sharpens iron, and one man sharpens another." The way iron sharpens iron, so to speak, is how a mentor can sharpen our faith in challenging us to grow and mature in Christ. Mentorship provides wisdom and advice. Having journeyed on the way of faith for a bit longer, the mentor will have the ability to share all this invaluable insight and advice that comes from experience. This is important when there is spiritual uncertainty or when one is met with very important and trying decisions. So, Proverbs 19:20–21 goes on to remind us, "Listen to advice and accept instruction, that you may gain wisdom in the future. Many are the plans in the mind of a man, but it is the purpose of the Lord that will stand." By seeking a counselor's advice, we consequently gain wisdom to take us through the complexities of life—that is, in decision-making for the purposes of God.

Thirdly, mentorship provides encouragement and support. It is paramount in these challenges that come with the Christian walk. There are instances when one may feel down, weak, and overpowered, and a mentor should always be there to give encouragement and support to sail through. In 1 Thessalonians 5:11, Paul pleads with these believers to "encourage one another and build one another up, just as you are doing." A mentor builds us up and reminds us of God's promises. This helps one to put on the shoes of the gospel and eyes on the Lord Jesus Christ while going through trials. To all these advantages one also has the place mentorship provides for the sake of personal growth and development. He'll help us to begin locating those areas in our lives in which we must grow and give us the tools, resources, and equipping necessary to enable such growth. Growth is at the heart of our relationship with

Christ, whereby we are called to be like Him. In this regard, the word of God avers, "But speaking the truth in love, we may grow up in all things into Him who is the head." Under a godly mentor, we can be instructed to apply the word of God into our lives in thinking, in prayer, and in living.

On the other hand, one must be careful not to suppose that mentoring is sidereal but mutual. For us to be faithful, we too must learn to grow in our faith, as the people we mentor make faithful investments in those around them. 2 Timothy 2:2 says, "And what you have heard from me in the presence of many witnesses entrust to faithful men who will be able to teach others also." This verse alone makes the reference that those things gained need to be passed on to another. This still further allows the whole circle of disciple making to continue on, strengthening the body of Christ. Not always this will be in the form of formalized relationships; it could be something like a church community or small group. More so, it becomes important to get people who are spiritually older, thus able to guide us and encourage us in growing. But, on the other hand, we should be available for others to mentor, to be able to share our experiences and insights that might help them in growth with Christ. The deep thing about mentoring may be that it reflects the mentoring relationship Christ had with his disciples. Jesus spent three years mentoring his disciples: He taught and set them right as he prepared them for the ministry they would undertake after his ascension. In the book of John, after washing His disciples' feet, Jesus says, "For I have given you an example that you also should do just as I have done to you." This example of servant leadership and mentorship laid the path for us to tread in our case of mentoring others in their walk with Christ.

Further, mentorship is a very practical way of expressing God's love and care toward His people. As 1 John 4:7 states, "Beloved, let us love one another, for love is from God, and whoever loves has been born of God and knows God." This means that we can express God's love to one another by nurturing the lives of people with godly love, helping others to grow and flourish in their walk with Christ. It strengthens the faith of the mentee and deepens that of the mentor, for in the twinkling eyes of people coming to know their Savior is joy. Spiritual guidance via a mentor is a very potent way to build a functional relationship with Christ. A mentor provides accountability, wisdom, and encouragement at the table. Keep us growing in faith, overcoming—in short, all those things that might come at us within our spiritual walk. A mentor teaches us principles of biblical discipleship and servant leadership much like Jesus did. Mentorship aids us in the discovery and realization of ways through which we may mature our walk with Christ, grow in knowledge of His Word, and come to be more like Him. Moreover, in mentoring, we are investing in the lives of others for the up building of the body of Christ and extending His kingdom. At the bottom line, however, mentorship is a gift of God to us for growing in faith and calling as followers of Christ.

CHAPTER SIX
THE THIRD PERSON

"How come we shy away from the Holy Spirit for the purpose of his coming, His primary assignment was to address darkness."

The Holy Spirit characterizes functional relationship with Christ and lies at the very core of Christianity. He is God within us and ideally should lead believers into a closer intimacy with Jesus. Any relation that one has with Him should be understood first with the exploration of who or what is the Holy Spirit, upon which follows a detailed exposition of his role in the life of a Christian.

THE PERSONALITY OF THE HOLY SPIRIT

The Holy Spirit also is a Person in the Trinity, coequal and coeternal with the Father and the Son. The doctrine of the Trinity lies at the heart of Christian theology, though it is complex and mysterious. The Holy Spirit was not something impersonal, like a force or some manifestation of power from God, but a Person to whom intellect, emotions, and will belonged. As a matter of fact, both are attributes of the Holy Spirit: personality, as well as deity, is borne witness in the Scripture. For instance, when Jesus says in John 14:26, "He is the Helper, the Holy Spirit, whom the Father will send in my name to teach you all things and to call to mind everything that I have said to you." To begin with, the very calling "Helper" testifies to the fact that the personality of the Holy Spirit works in supplication on behalf of the believer in their active lives. The apostle Peter identifies that lying to the Holy Spirit clearly means lying to God in Acts 5:3-4, further identifying that the Spirit is divine. Some characteristics ascribed to God alone are ascribed to the Holy Spirit. Such can be said about Him being omnipresent. David proved that there is no place through which he could really be free from the presence of the Spirit. He is omniscient; it is He who knows the thoughts of God and has revealed them to us. Further, the Holy Spirit is eternal. He was called the "eternal Spirit" in Hebrews 9:14. The full recognition of the Holy Spirit as fully divine and a person can be appreciated only when one considers His essential role in developing a workable relationship with Christ. He is not, therefore, an agency of God's will but a person who comes to relate Himself to us, to change us, and to bring us more and more into relation with Jesus.

HOW THE HOLY SPIRIT MAKES CHRIST REAL TO US

In relating to Christ, the Holy Spirit touches upon every matter related to the life of a Christian: conversion, sanctification, and even glorification. From the point of being converted, through sanctification and even glorification, it is through the Holy Spirit that the believer is made to come closer to Christ by what Christ has done in them and through them.

HOLY SPIRIT AND REGENERATION

Regeneration is perhaps the first and foremost activity of the Holy Spirit in the life of a believer. That is why Jesus thought it so vital a process, yea, so vital, that he considered it could not take place in the life of one that desired seeing and entering into the views of the kingdom of the godhead: "Ye must be born again of the Spirit." This new birth is not symbolic or metaphorical but is deep, deep, in the core of the spiritual graveyard, through the powerful initial change that translates a believer from spiritual death unto life with Christ himself. Titus 3:5 says, "Not by works of righteousness which we have done, but according to his mercy he saved us, by the washing of regeneration and renewal of the Holy Ghost." This is what the Holy Ghost actually does: cleanses man from all his sins and gives a right relationship with Christ. But for the regenerating work of the Holy Ghost, we should to this day be dead in trespasses and sins, and God's call could not be answered, neither could we at that time accept the offered life in Christ.

THE HOLY SPIRIT AND CONVICTION OF SIN

This has to come before getting into a relationship with Christ, where it would be a knowledge of the need for Christ. This is working through the Holy Spirit, convicting us in the areas of sin, righteousness, and judgment. The Holy Spirit shows us the areas in our lives in which we need to work on, not to condemn us but rather to help us repent and build in us a better and stronger follower of Christ. Conviction of sin is, therefore, quite necessary in the process of salvation. Our eyes are opened to the Holy Spirit and to our sinful condition, with which there is nothing for which we can save ourselves. Our conscience becomes sensitive and sentient with the heavy burden of sin, beginning to seek forgiveness and redemption in Christ. It is through this convicting work of the Holy Spirit, for without it we would be utterly blind to our spiritual state and incapable of fathoming the seriousness of our sins or the necessity of Christ's sacrifice.

HOLY SPIRIT AND SANCTIFICATION

Sanctification is the process whereby the believer is led through in being conformed to the image of Christ. It is throughout life and continuous, with the action of the

Holy Spirit being concomitant. As inscribed by Paul in the second letter to the Thessalonians, "But we ought always to thank God for you, brothers and sisters loved by the Lord, because God chose you as first fruits to be saved through the sanctifying work of the Spirit and through belief in the truth." It is the Holy Spirit who makes us gradually mature into Christ's likeness, hence leading us to the defeat of sin, renewal of our minds, and the production of his fruits among us. That is the experience of transformation that keeps us in living relationship with him: He draws us close and transforms the desires of our hearts so they are congruent with his will.

THE HOLY SPIRIT AND GOD'S WORD

During the study of the word of God, it is the Holy Spirit who guides a believer through John 16:13 in all truth. He will open up their hearts and mind towards the understanding of the Scripture in such a way that deep spiritual truth will be unfolded in the life of a person to bring them closer to Christ. Our perception of the Word would have been shallow were it not for the guidance of the Holy Spirit. This badly hampers one's relationship with Jesus.

THE HOLY SPIRIT AND PRAYER

Prayer is right at the center of a believer's relationship with Christ, and the Holy Spirit plays a very great role in the lives of believers with regard to the same. Romans 8:26-27 says, "In the same way, the Spirit helps us in our weakness. We do not know what we ought to pray for, but the Spirit himself intercedes for us through wordless groans. And he who searches our hearts knows the mind of the Spirit, because the Spirit intercedes for God's people in accordance with the will of God." In this our inability, the Holy Ghost helps us. For instance, we don't know what God wants us to pray for. But the Holy Spirit prays for us with groanings that cannot be articulated in words. He intercedes in our pleading, so divine intercession is the assurance that our pleading will indeed fall in line with God's purposes; our requests will be in harmony with His will. This is the core of relationship with Christ because it develops our communion with Him and keeps the rhythm of His plans. It is the Holy Spirit who also fills our prayers with power. In fact, Jude 1:20 teaches that it is necessary for a Christian to "pray in the Holy Spirit," meaning he has to rely upon the Holy Spirit to lead and to empower him in the prayer. So when a believer prays, especially in the Spirit, his prayer will then be with the power of God; hence, the prayer is effective and has the power of transforming a life.

HOLY SPIRIT AND SERVICE

Functional relationship with Christ does not apply only to personal spiritual growth but to Hebraic service to others in love and Great Commission. It is through the Holy Spirit that one is empowered for service, spiritually gifting believers for the edification of the Church and moving toward the kingdom of God. "But you will receive power when the Holy Spirit comes on you, and you will be my witnesses in Jerusalem, and in all Judea and Samaria, and to the ends of the earth"—even Jesus said this about His disciples in Acts 1:8. This, however, is not the usual human power; rather, it is divine enablement for the believer to preach the Gospel with great boldness, put across a miracle, and serve humbly for the sake of Christ. The spiritual gifts are given to believers by the will of the Holy Spirit for the common benefit of the edification of the Body of Christ and the service in ministry. That is, when one is given teaching, another prophecy, another healing, or administration—all these works of Spirit power evident in Jesus' serving come to work in us to enable us to serve him in the same way. We have no strength to live an effective Christian life unless one relies on the force of the Holy Spirit in us through His gracious moving and working. He enables us to do the work at the behest of God so that our relationship with Christ will bear fruit in reality.

THE HOLY SPIRIT AND ASSURANCE OF SALVATION

It is important in relation to the assurance of salvation and the role of the Holy Spirit in this relationship with Christ on account of which Paul is emphasizing that "The Spirit himself testifies with our spirit that we are included in God's family." It is this inner witness emanating from the Holy Spirit that shall guarantee feelings of security in the relationship of the believer with Christ. It is very important in having a functional relationship with Christ that assurance of such salvation be ensured. It will make a person be confident in coming before God with the knowledge that, in Christ, they are accepted. Under unsuitable circumstances or when going through mature spiritual warfare, the Holy Spirit continually assures your heart of God's love and faithfulness. Not on our feelings, not on our performance, but on the unchanging promises of God. The Holy Spirit has sealed us for the day of redemption, and it is that and nothing else that guarantees our inheritance in Christ. The sealing of the Spirit is God's own mark of ownership, evidence that we are His, and our salvation is sure.

HOLY SPIRIT AND SPIRITUAL WARFARE

Spiritual warfare is the brand of Christian life. The believer is pitched in unending battle with the powers of darkness. The Holy Ghost has been left to equip us as warriors for this struggle with the weaponry of God and the spiritual strength to withstand Satan's deployment against us. Continuing, the Ephesians 6:10-18 describes the armor of God: for every combatant of Christ, there is a goading into the equipping of him with a belt of truth; breastplate of righteousness; shield of faith; helmet of salvation; sword of the Spirit, which is the Word of God; and the gospel of peace, which is sandals. And this armor can be put on only by the Holy Ghost, and the ability for the handling of the sword is enabled.

THE HOLY SPIRIT AND CONVICTIONS: A PART WAY TO HEALING

You are more or less behaving like you are in fear, anxiety, and illusion of the Holy Spirit, most of all the feeling that they live in darkness. You run away from the Holy Spirit because you reason you are unworthy to be in His presence due to their misdeeds, sins, or weight of spiritual and moral failings. This really is a misconception of the modality and nature of the Holy Spirit's purpose. The reverse is quite the truth: It is precisely to meet this darkness within us that the Holy Spirit comes to brood over, bringing light and life as at the beginning. One of the things that man has been wired to is hiding himself from something that reveals his flaws and weaknesses. This is very true in spiritual matters. Jesus said, "This is the condemnation: the light has come into the world, but men loved darkness rather than light because their deeds were evil. For everyone who does evil hates the light, and does not come to the light, lest his deeds should be exposed." In fact, many have a feeling that He will expose them; it is their conviction, and they are afraid of the Holy Spirit. They almost come to understand, during their lifetime, that the degree of sin inside is probably too deep for the Holy Spirit to convict them of it. They even fear that the Holy Spirit would come under judgment, show them more about the sins they are involved in than they themselves are conscious of, and leave them in a worse state than they are actually aware of. Such fear can then instill a kind of spiritual paralysis: the individual, ensnared by darkness, fails to approach the light for fear of what the light might reveal.

So, it becomes necessary that any understanding of the real work of the Holy Spirit really must go back to the beginning, to the very first record of the Spirit of God in the Bible. It says in Genesis 1:2 that the earth "was formless and empty, darkness was over the surface of the deep, and the Spirit of God was hovering over the waters." Here we have an intricate picture and, at the same time, a deep one: there was the earth in chaos; that is to say, it was without form, it was void, and it was in darkness. And the Spirit of God was hovering over the face of the waters. The indwelling Holy Spirit has come not to condemn or judge, but to accomplish what He had done in the chaos of creation: to bring light, order, and life. In the way He did while hovering over the disorder of creation, just about to bring forth light upon the commandment of God that is the way, He comes to us who are in the dark. Surely he does not cringe before the sliminess of what is inside of us, but neither does he get mired in it, for he at once transfigures it into something lovely and life-giving. He is the Holy Spirit who fills these formless and void spaces of our selves: our own sin, despair and brokenness. This means that the Holy Spirit will come to blow life into that space, bringing light where before there was just darkness.

The Holy Ghost has set out to light up our lives, our minds, and our hearts in order that He will illuminate us with a real view and walk in the light. Indeed, according to the promise of Jesus, in John 16:13: "But when he, the Spirit of truth, comes, he will guide you into all the truth." The guidance of the Holy Spirit has been like a light along one's path, guiding one in the way to walk through life's affairs and entanglements with wisdom and knowledge. Though not switched on to merely light the way, it is in light that we are changed. Now, when the Holy Spirit lays his light on the darkness inside of us, he doesn't do it to condemn us; he does it to heal us and to restore us. But Ephesians 5:13-14 says, "When anything is exposed and reproved by the light, it is made visible and clear, and where everything is visible and clear, there is light. That is why it is said, 'Wake up, sleeper, rise from the dead, and Christ will shine on you.'" The Holy Ghost shines in men's hearts; He wakes men from their spiritual sleep, lifts them from the deadness of sin, and gets them into glorious light in Christ.

In fleeing from the Holy Ghost because of their darkness, after all they flee from that very Light which alone could save them, a Light that had power to disperse that very darkness in them and to lead them out of the powers of darkness into a place of freedom and life. That that most compassionate luminescence should be reached for with optimism and faith and not with dread is the sad irony of this scenario.

Why is it that most persons will do anything to avoid

coming close to the Holy Spirit? The answer is because most of us fear His convicting work. Most all of these people do not understand what conviction is, and they think it is actually condemnation. Thus, they stay as far away from the Holy Spirit due to fear of thinking bad about their selves. Condemnation has nothing to do with conviction, but it is a major part of the healing process. John 16:8 says, "And when he comes, he will convict the world concerning sin and judgment and righteousness." Godly conviction, the work of the Holy Spirit, is meant to be that which does not in any way drive us away from God but, rather, draws us to God. Conviction from the Holy Spirit is meant to bring forth the realization that it may be time for adjustment in some area of one's life. It is an invitation from the darkness into the light of God. Holy Spirit conviction convinces with forgiveness and renewal. The believer is secure in 1 John 1:9: "If we confess our sins, He is faithful and just to forgive us our sins and to cleanse us from all unrighteousness." Put in other words, the Holy Spirit convicts to bring one to the place where confession is possible, from which cleansing is possible, through Christ alone. The conviction of the Holy Spirit becomes a place where God in the believing Christian works, leading us unto the healing and freeing of our souls that we are so in great need of.

How the Holy Spirit ministers to us to bring renewal is very powerful. The Holy Spirit does not just come over into our lives and leave it at that. Instead, He has been about the business of renewal and transformation, where He is progressively making us conformed to the image of Christ. It is this rediscovery that the Apostle Paul meant much later when he wrote in 2 Corinthians 3:18, "So all of us who have had that veil removed can see and reflect the glory of the Lord. And the Lord—who is the Spirit—makes us more and more like him as we are changed into his glorious image." No, not a night makeover but a lifetime one. Better still, it is what the Holy Spirit does within us, much of the time in the most secret and dark places of our hearts, to change our lives into divinely guided glory. Light being changed through the Holy Spirit is light changing from inside. We resist this process of change, for it is too painful; much of the work of the Holy Spirit is about confrontation with very painful facts about us and about deeply surrendering deeply implanted patterns of sin and brokenness. Actually, it is a necessary part of healing in that very pain. The Holy Spirit really shows the darkness lurking inside us, not to shame us but to liberate us.

INVITING THE HOLY SPIRIT INTO OUR DARKNESS

Certainly, in making space for the Holy Spirit to renew us, we must truly make serious room for Him even in the deepest recesses of our darkness. It is in these places that some of our attitudes and views may need to be transformed in seeing the Holy Spirit for what it truly is: an influx of divine aid arriving precisely when we need it. The Holy Ghost is nothing else but the Comforter standing for our defense since he is the Paraclete: the one who goes to go along with, to guide, to strengthen. It is not appalled, and it never is repelled by our darkness, but it just goes right in, because it is to bring light and life that He has come. For He never gets startled; He is never dismayed by our darkness, but it just goes right in, for it is always to bring light and life that He has come. Of this he says in another one of his Psalms, "If I say, 'surely the darkness will hide me and the light become night around me,' even the darkness will not be dark to you; the night will shine like the day, for darkness is as light to you." He, by means of His Holy Spirit, sees right through our darkness. And there is nothing so dark that to Him it may not just as well be light; yea, literally, He can change into the times through which growth and healing and transformation shine at last. One of the most magnificent ministries of the Holy Spirit is the hope He pours into our lives. He cannot so easily be compromised by that sense of hopelessness, that sense of defeat, when we feel ourselves trapped in the blackness of darkness. He comes to us right in the face of our overwhelming sin, failure, and brokenness when the weight of all of that, which convinces us we can't change, tells us we are unredeemable in and of ourselves. He approaches with a message from the Holy Spirit: no darkness is dark enough that the light of Christ cannot shine upon it.

And again wrote the Apostle Paul to the church in Rome, "May the God of hope fill you with all joy and peace as you trust in him so that you may overflow with hope by the power of the Holy Spirit." It is the Holy Spirit who carries on bringing in the overflow and the flooding of our hearts with great expectancy and assurance that God can be asked or thought to do exceedingly more exactly as one can ask of, than one thinks of, repercussions exceedingly abundantly. But it is He who stands at the point of view and gives us the strength to hold out, the courage to face our darkness, and faith to believe that true change can indeed happen. It is a dread-based response, when in our fear of the dark and what it conceals, we flee from the Holy Spirit. But doesn't the Holy Spirit come for what—for the very darkness resident within us to brood over us, just as he brooded over the earth at the beginning of time?

INTRODUCTION

CHAPTER SEVEN
NOT DASH BUT A MARATHON

*"Oftentimes we fall because
we want to bump into Growth."*

He went on his knees beside his bed, crying in the dark, throwing himself about up and down on the floor with his faith; he had been such a strong believer, and for years now he had been searching with his heart for God; now he wore down under its weight, and tired, he prayed in one last desperate whisper, wondering when he could continue. He wondered if it were usual to feel so tired in his quest for a deeper acquaintance with God. In a way, feeling like an utter human being burdened by the facts of life and the powerlessness of his muscles John did. He was standing alone, weary, and living through one of the most basic elements of humanity: the struggle to grow in faith, a journey distinguished by exhaustion and renewal alike.

It is not surprising at all that one tires out or even

becomes disheartened in the pursuit of a functional relationship with Christ. What kind of exhaustion this state of affairs has does not show how weak or failures a person is, but on the contrary, the genuine humanness of a person. Finite as we are, sometimes we do get tired, more so in our journey with God, where demands of growth and rigors of life press heavily on us. Not to yield to fatigue is a thing, but to recognize it as something quite natural in the process of spiritual maturity. This growth will not all come at once, as if by magic, but growing in steady steps forward should follow, much like a baby learns to walk, until the full maturity in Christ is reached. Truly, much of the literature compares the process of spiritual growth with that of a child growing up. Well, just like a newborn who always needs nourishment, care, and guidance, so we in this faith-growing process too need spiritual nourishment once in a while. This is the dimension of nourishment, and it would seem that this God-is-Mother metaphor is best to catch a tender, caring, patient relationship God has with us. We, in the person of Jesus Christ, know the divine full nurturing through his long-suffering guiding and teaching toward spiritual maturity.

Beginning at Genesis and running throughout to the Revelation, there is a metaphor of God as a nourishing person. This is illustrated by the words of God to the prophet in Isaiah 66:13, "As one whom his mother comforts, so I will comfort you; you shall be comforted in Jerusalem." It is this verse that brings out the maternal aspect of God's care, where the simile equates His comfort to the comfort a mother gives a child. This is nurture not of the comforting variety in times of trouble only but one which steers and guides us through life's challenges, letting us grow and mature our faith. Jesus during His time on earth represented this nurturing aspect of God. Often, He referred to Himself as being descriptive of His role caretaker and provider. In Matthew 23:37, Jesus mourns for Jerusalem, saying, "How often would I have gathered your children together, even as a hen gathers her chicks beneath her wings, but you would not have it!" Now, He uses something the actions of the mother hen in caring for her chicks to say just how much He wants to keep safe and care for those who come to Him. The passage thus unveils Christ's sorrow, at the same time, for the rejection of His care and the enduring love, with the readiness of embracing it in nurturing them, despite all the resistances.

A Christian's faith is unrushed, it is not a dash but a marathon. It calls for staying power, patience, and above all, faith in the care of God. All of us are as dependent on Christ's helping arm as a little child learning how to walk is on his mother, for passing through all the predicaments of spiritual development. To be too tired or too discouraged to go on is not a spiritual failure; rather, on the contrary, it is testimony that we are human; therein, in fact, lies the need for God's sustaining grace to keep moving forward. Ephesians 4:15 has the believers growing "up in every way into him who is the head, into Christ." Growth does not occur in a single day; on the contrary, it's a progressive occurrence that needs time, effort, and nourishment by God's presence in one's life. Similar to how an infant passes through different stages, so are we grown into our relationship with Christ. There are moments when we feel very strong, filled with faith, and moments when we feel weak and weary. Both of these are part of the normal process of journeying and call for trust in God's continuous presence and guidance.

One deep example of God as nurture is taken from the relationship of Christ to His twelve disciples. Jesus spent three years exhibiting these: teaching, guiding, and nurturing the disciples. He knew that they were like spiritual infants that have to constantly be fed, like children that need to be taken care of and taught. Yes, Jesus was far more patient and compassionate even when they stumbled or when they simply could not understand. Yes, He did correct them in love and encouraged them to continue in their growth of faith. Discipleship is not instant perfectness but gradual growth—step by step—through which these disciples mature in their relationship with Christ.

In John 15:1-2, Jesus takes the metaphor of vine and branches to relate Himself and His followers: "I am the vine, the true one; and my Father is the vinedresser. And every branch that bears fruit, he prunes, that it may bear more fruit." Or, in several ways, this passage does somewhat stress the nurturing and growth of a life in Christ. The process is painful at times, wherein pruning is necessary in order to produce more fruit, just like the trials and challenges to overcome for a spiritual journey towards growth and maturity. Also, we have to take note that spiritual growth is not only our duty, but it is also God's and ours. There is an amazingly beautiful commandment in Philippians 2:12-13: "Therefore, my beloved, as you have always obeyed, so now, not only as in my presence but much more in my absence, work out your own salvation with fear and trembling, for it is God who works in you, both to will and to work for his good pleasure." As much as we are commanded to pursue our spiritual growth vigorously, so are we reminded that He is the One who enables us and tends to us, working in us to perform whatever pleases Him. In such moments of spiritual exhaustion, one has to be replenished by God. But in Isaiah 40:31, there is an equally forceful promise: "But they that wait upon the Lord shall renew their strength; they shall mount up with wings as eagles; they shall run, and not be weary; and they shall walk, and not faint." It reminds us that the source of our strength is not in the doing but in the waiting upon the Lord Himself, trusting His ability to keep us through the many ups and downs of the journey. For it is in this waiting, this resting totally on God's nurture, that we gather strength to go on growing, step by step, until the due time when we will reach maturity in Christ.

The motherhood of God in Christ is the essence of his dealing with the life and growth of the church; it reminds one that their spiritual growth does not have to be something that they do alone. Then, just like the mother does for her child, so God first gives grace and every other required supply for development in the faith. It is not such nourishment that comes only at our weakest moments but such nourishment that is constantly there to support us in growth, even in channels we are too blind to identify. Spiritual maturity is a progressive process and, to that end, it is an invitation to patience not only for ourselves but also for God's timing. Some of those seasons will seem like times of rapid growth; others may feel like seasons of waiting. There will be times of clarity and times of confusion. In these seasons of our lives, we remain called to trust in the nurture of God, knowing He will finish what He has started through each of us. Philippians 1:6 reassures, "And I am sure of this, that he who began a good work in you will bring it to completion at the day of Jesus Christ."

We can also see the nurturing character of Christ in his understanding of our human limitations. In Matthew 11:28-30, Jesus states, "Come unto me, all ye that labor and are heavy laden, and I will give you rest. Take my yoke upon you, and learn from me, for I am tender and humble in heart, and you shall find rest for your souls. For my yoke is easy, and my burden is light." Now this text really brings out the sensitive heart of Christ, who does not deny us that which we have been working so hard at putting in front as the best of our works in order to earn His blessing. On the contrary, He calls us to be at peace, learn from Him, and grow under His care. He must bear in mind right at the moment one enters into a relationship with Christ that spiritual maturity is a journey and not an arrival. It is training in always wanting to know God more and more, changing because of His love, and expressing that character in your life. Definitely, this journey is filled with struggles, and you will sometimes feel like giving up. Indeed, it is at such moments that we are best disposed for God to nurture us and for Him to direct, comfort, and strengthen us in whichever way we can move forward.

Further identification of God's nurturing nature is through Christ, revealing the importance of the community in our spiritual development. Just as a child will need a family in his/her growth, so are we to have the support from the community of Christians to help us on our way. The Church should take the place of Christ's body, in which we can receive encouragement and accountability, but above all, in which we can be nurtured through the ministry of other believers. Hebrews 10:24-25 says, "And let us consider how to stir up one another to love and good works, not neglecting to meet together, as is the habit of some, but encouraging one another, and all the more as you see the Day drawing near." If we are to feel it out, we would easily faint in running. Through common life, we should be able to proceed in growth understanding that we are not running our race alone. This means that one gets tired and weary along the journey to a functional relationship with Christ. Moments of exhaustion are not failed moments, they show us how much yet human we are, and that we need the nurture of God Himself. The question that pops in our heads is that "What then should we be doing whilst being in this weak state?"

Indeed, on the spiritual journey, we turn out to be weak and get tired of the daily routines, even besieged by doubts. Such feelings are part of the typical experience and should not equate to failure or inadequacy. Just as feelings of weakness are normal, one ought to learn that our relationship with Christ can remain functional and even grow stronger despite all such challenges. Allowing us to fall back on God's supporting grace in our weakness means that practices to nurse our faith and strengthen our will are called for in the development of a living, lasting relationship with Christ.

PRAYER

Prayer is among the most important things helping one keep in a working relationship with Christ, even when a person is so weak. Prayer is like a lifeline through which we are connected to God. An individual can talk to God through prayer. He shares his needs and is given God's direction and power. It becomes our comfort and enhances our faith that we are not left alone when problems befall us. As the psalmist writes, "When the righteous cry for help, the Lord hears and delivers them out of all their troubles," as captured in Psalm 34:17. This would not be correct if it were reduced just to requesting for things in a prayer. It is more of an appeal to that deeper and much more intimate level of a relationship with God where we can pour each of our hearts out before God and begin to listen to His voice. In times of weakness, prayer within the heart of the believer should assume more importance as a means of drawing near to Christ. Even Jesus Christ showed the power of prayer at Gethsemane in the garden on the eve of His crucifixion when weakness was overwhelming. Fully aware of what lay ahead, Jesus prayed intently that he might have strength for the trials he was going to endure. Luke 22:44 says, "And being in agony, He prayed more earnestly; and His sweat became like great drops of blood falling down to the ground." In His humanity, Jesus felt a major burden of what was yet ahead, yet He—into the Father's face—looked in prayer for strength from a relationship with God. The example teaches us that, much more than an appeal to divine aid in times of weakness, prayer is the way for alignment of the will with God and finding strength to help overcome adversities.

THE WORD OF GOD

The Bible is literally God's revealed Word; it is wisdom, inspiration, truth, which kicks right into our hearts. When we are weak, it's the bread of life that feeds us to build our faith, so we can stand on God's promises. As spoken in Psalm 119:105, "Thy word is a lamp to my feet and a light to my path," just as the lamp illuminates the way in darkness, so does God's Word—scripture—give clarity, direction in times we are lost or overwhelmed. It is thus by reading and meditating on the word of God that God's promises and truths are distilled into our hearts, strengthening our faith. It is easy to believe we are weak when we are weak; it's easy to give in to thoughts, doubts, and fears. But balanced thinking on the right proportions of the Word of God counters these lies with truth about who God is and what He has done for us. Of this, for example, Paul was reminding us when he wrote that nothing will be able to separate us from the love of God in Christ Jesus our Lord (Romans 8L39). It is this kind of assurance about God's unchanging love that acts like a powerful anchor, holding the relationship with Christ in place, even when one feels very weak.

DEPENDENCE ON GOD

So often, especially in our spiritual walk, the greatest challenge is stepping out to do things in the strength of our own flesh rather than in the power and provision of God. But in weakness His strength is made perfect. Writing to the Corinthians, Paul wrote the divine response to his pleading for the removal of a "thorn in the flesh," located in 2 Corinthians 12:9: "My grace is sufficient for you; for my power is made perfect in weakness." Accordingly, it was in this truth that he could say: "Therefore I will boast all the more gladly of my weaknesses, so that the power of Christ may rest upon me." In connection to our relationship with Christ, humility recognizes our limitations in regard to us not being able to keep it on our own. It calls us to lay aside pride and our tendency towards self-reliance and to bank totally on God's grace. A disposition of this nature is the one that more perfectly binds us to Christ but also opens us to His power and strength in our weakness. Through dependence on God we learn to receive His sustaining grace that delves into trust for Him and reliance on His unfailing love.

THE COMMUNITY OF BELIEVERS

Another important part of an active relationship with the Lord is being involved with other people who belong to Him. The Christian life was not to be lived in isolation. Rather, we are called to be a part of the body of Christ, which enables us to draw support, encouragement, and accountability. Fellow Christians envelope us with their prayer, exhortation, and walking together in times when we are weak. "And let us consider one another to provoke unto love and to good works, not forsaking the assembling of ourselves together, as the manner of some is; but exhorting one another: and so much the more, as ye see the day approaching" (Hebrews 10:25). The body provides the Christian opportunity to bear one another's burdens, as Paul urges us in Galatians 6:2, "Bear one another's burdens, and so fulfill the law of Christ." The least thing we can do is stand on our feet in feebleness as a result of the assistance and prayers of believers lifted on our behalf, pointing us back in thankfulness to the faithfulness of God. Not only is there a list of ways we serve others in community other than through counseling, but serving others bolsters our relationship with Christ too. The more we serve and love others, the more we are reminded of the example Christ set for us, and the closer He leads us to Himself.

WORSHIP

Worship is not about Sunday-morning sing-along or attending church but the way of living in such ways that one would honor and bring glory to God in every detail. Furthermore, when one is weak, worship helps the soul of that particular person to shift focus from problems onto the greatness of God. Worship in the time of trouble is the opportunity the acts of worship provide for a person to magnify God as sovereign, good, and faithful even when circumstances turn hard. Now in Acts 16, we have one wonderful example of worship in the context of weakness. Paul and Silas were whipped, put in prison, chained, yet chose to worship God in their desolate condition. Acts 16:25 says, "About midnight Paul and Silas were praying and singing hymns to God, and the prisoners were listening to them." So, in the middle of all of their sufferings, Paul and Silas turned their hearts toward God in worship, and that became testifying praise to all of the others who were around them in such a way that miraculously the chains fell off them, and that jailer and his whole family came to faith in Christ. This story reminds us that, at times, it is through worship that chains of discouragement and despair are broken and spirits are lifted to higher levels in God. But this will not be enough: corporate worship, going with fellow believers for times of praise and honor of God together, is also such an imperative necessity. Corporate worship allows us to come together as the body of Christ, lifting our voices together in unison and really experiencing the palpable presence of God. "But you are holy, enthroned on the praises of Israel," as Psalm 22:3 declares. As we come together in worship, an atmosphere is created by which God's manifested presence brings peace, joy, and strength into our lives.

FASTING

Another spiritual discipline that we can perform to maintain our relationship with Christ, especially during periods of weakness, is fasting. Basically, fasting involves an abstention from food or other natural needs during a period of time to draw near to God in search of Him. Fasting is not a way of twisting God's arm to act in favor of us or to force His hand to do what we will, but it is an appeal to God in a humble way to seek dependency with hearts drawn to His purposes. He talked about fasting in Matthew 6:16-18: "And when you fast, do not look gloomy like the hypocrites, for they disfigure their faces that their fasting may be seen by others. Truly I say to you, they have received their reward. But when you fast, anoint your head and wash your face that your fasting may not be seen by others but by your Father who is in secret. And your Father who sees in secret will reward you." So fasting, when genuinely done in the right heart, could bring a person closer to God and renew spiritual strength, clearing up and bringing directions regarding our walk with Christ.

THE SPEAKING OF WORDS

Confession and repentance of sins are another important practice for keeping the relationship working with Christ. Our sins are what start to wall up between us and God, shutting off the relationship. But when confession and repentance are done, one will re-open fellowship with Christ and therefore be forgiven and cleansed by Him. As 1 John 1:9 presents, "If we confess our sins, He is faithful and just to forgive us our sins and to cleanse us from all unrighteousness." Confession does not imply mere acknowledgment but rather turning away from sin and toward God. In fact, repentance itself literally has to do with a change of mind and heart whereby one chooses to turn from sin unto righteousness. It is through the looking glass of humility and repentance that we find God's grace and mercy: "Draw near to God and He will draw near to you. Cleanse your hands, you sinners; and purify your hearts, you double-minded".

CHAPTER EIGHT
NOTHING TO LOSE!

"If it was not true, he would have not died! There is nothing to lose!"

This, of course, speaks so deeply to the Christian faith that we have nothing to lose by following Christ. This is where one does the calculus in a cost-benefit kind of way of what one does; following Jesus Christ seems to offer a call into ultimate having in which true loss is really impossible. This will be according to the Scriptures, borne along by the redemptive dynamic of the Gospel: "In Christ we already have everything we need for life and godliness." The reality that we literally have nothing to lose in following Christ reigns during the promise of eternal life: "For God so loved the world that He gave His one and only Son, that whoever believes in Him shall not perish but have eternal life." This providence of eternal life is the big gain to every believer, far greater than all loss that can be sustained in this world. He repeated it in one of his letters, "For to me, to live is Christ and to die is gain" (Philippians 1:21). For

Paul, this faith in Christ meant, even in this earthly life, that death was not a loss but gain; the door into eternal life in the presence of God. And, all temporal struggles, sacrifices, and sufferings of this life, in Romans 8:18, amount to nothing when weighed against the glory coming in eternity. So many times when we felt that to live for Christ was going to rob us of so much in life, it is actually He who gives us life eternal existence, relationship with God, and a place in His Kingdom.

THE ABUNDANT LIFE IN CHRIST

Though with the assurance of eternal life, following Jesus results in abundance of life here on earth. Jesus said, "The thief comes only to steal, kill, and destroy; I came that they may have life, and have it abundantly" (John 10:10). The abundant life in Christ means more than material wealth and passing success. He is a life overflowing with the presence of God, the riches of peace, joy, and purpose. Christ gives deep transformation. It is held that in Him alone life in its fullness and richness is seen. We are no longer slaves unto sin, fear, and the empty pursuit of the things of this earth. Right relationships with God bring real freedom, life purpose, and satisfaction. As found in Galatians 5:22-23, first, the fruit that the Spirit brings is a great increase in life, full of love, peace, patience, kindness, goodness, faithfulness, gentleness, and self-control—all that emanates from the manifest presence of God. In fact, those are referred to as the things that increase our lives in a way so enriched that even through them, money, power, and worldly pleasure cannot bring forth.

Yes, to follow Jesus will cost you something, but the price is nothing to what the alternative cost. In fact, He put it in this way Himself: "For what does it profit a man to gain the whole world, and lose his own soul? Or what will a man give in exchange for his soul?" Very certainly, if in the gaining of the things in the world's possession we lose the friendship of God, we have lost everything. For in the end, we shall be distant from Him. Holy Scriptures to the contrary, specifically pointing out a reaction for a person who rejects Christ. In John 3:36, it is stated: "Whoever believes in the Son has eternal life. Whoever rejects the Son will not see life, because the wrath of God remains upon him." To drive the point even further, a person who fails in his belief in or acceptance of Christ will miss eternal life and subsequently suffer the wrath of God. In following Christ, however, we are definitely saved from that judgment and brought into precisely the same fullness of life that was meant for us.

TEMPORAL LOSSES OF THIS LIFE

This is one of the fears that keeps so many from all-out surrender to Christ—the vague and at times quite palpable loss of fun, friendship, or status. Scripture puts it in perspective: "The world and its desires pass away, but whoever does the will of God lives forever," he says. So what loss are we talking about for now in comparison with the reward that is eternal in serving Christ? The question we ask here is definitely answered by Jesus himself in existence in Matthew 19:29, "He that hath forsaken houses, or, brothers or sisters or father, mother, wife, children, or lands for my sake shall receive a hundred fold and shall inherit life everlasting." For whatever we have left behind—for Christ's sake, Jesus makes a clear promise—we will have a full return in this life and the life to come, manifold. For we lose absolutely nothing in everything; on the contrary, what we invest is in a future that is secure and full of glory, immeasurably.

GOD'S PROVISION IS SURE

The other reason is that we have nothing to lose under Christ because we are assured of His provision. Jesus taught his disciples not to worry about their needs. "But seek first the kingdom of God and his righteousness, and all these things shall be added to you" (Matthew 6:33). We shall not leave priority attachment to God and His kingdom; so many other things, material and otherwise, will be provided and taken care of by Him. This faith in God's supply has been further bolstered by the words of the apostle Paul himself: "And my God shall supply all your need, according to His riches in glory, by Christ Jesus." How our need is fulfilled by God in ways surpassing our conception can comfort us and free us from fear of something lacking because of our choice to Christ. Be it material self-provision, self-sufficiency in emotions, or fueling spiritually, God sure does not forget to provide for His children, and that is what makes his love incomparable to any other. There is some kind of dynamism in coming to Christ, which is at the core, and that is the love of Christ.

Apostle Paul summarized it well: "For I am persuaded that neither death nor life, nor angels nor principalities nor powers, neither things present nor things to come, neither height nor depth, nor any other creature shall be able to separate us from the love of God, which is in Christ Jesus our Lord." So, it is unconditional, irrevocable, and an all-encompassing kind of love. It is in Christ that man's deepest longing finds satisfaction: his security and affirmation, which he is longing for. Compare that now to this treasure of the love of Christ that is of immeasurably worth more than any other in this life. In following Christ there is absolutely nothing at a loss; rather, we can gain the best ever that could be given to us—His love. It is a love that will never let one go, that will hold one through every trial, keep one through every sorrow, and make one's soul precious as a child of God. Nothing is lost with Christ—only gained—that one gives oneself over to the light of such truths.

Then come "fears and doubts"; these are "fears and doubts that would keep me from responding" to Him with the promise of eternal life, abundant living, and unshakeable love in Christ. Truly, what we give up for Him is but temporal—a fact that each one of us must remember well. If we are afraid of what we might lose, then those are nothing in the light of what we will gain: the priceless treasures of knowing and being known by Christ. We accept the call of death-to-life discipleship, take one hesitant step after another, and find pathways that are abundant and purposeful, life-giving, and life-saving, fearless and confident in the God who, in love and provision, truly will hold the future in the palm of his hand. In Christ, one loses nothing but gains all.

ABOUT THE AUTHOR

Prince Jeremiah Sackey, overseer of Chosen and Royal Ministries, which operates in Dallas, Texas, New York, and Africa, is committed to bringing people closer to God via his preaching and writing. He is also the founder and president of ISIT (In Spirit In Truth), a fast-growing Christian social networking app accessible for free on the Apple and Google Play stores. This platform, created to unite the body of Christ, provides a clean and regulated area that inspires, motivates, and amplifies Christian perspectives in a social media world that is frequently dominated by negativity and offensive content. He and his wife, Shalaine Faith Sackey, are both excellent in inspiring others to pursue greatness in Christ through character and words.

 pastorpsackey@gmail.com

 Apostle Jeremiah Sackey

 Chosen And Royal Ministries

CONCLUSION

Jesus said in Matthew 24:14, "And this gospel of the kingdom will be preached in all the world as a witness to all the nations and then the end will come." There are many great men and women of God, ministers of the gospel around the world laboring and risking their lives to ensure that this scripture above is fully fulfilled, that souls are drawn from the kingdom of darkness into the marvelous light of Jesus. Yet there are also many false prophets who are wolves in sheep clothing as Jesus said, trying very hard with schemes to lure people into darkness, including believers who are genuinely seeking God. Today, in our dark world, you hear they are inventing new ways of seeking and serving the Lord like New Age, psychic practices, divinations, occulted practices, witchcraft, and various new religions all in the name of one God. Countless numbers of Christians have been misled into bondage and darkness, and many are quitting or giving up on going to church and in faith overall because of the many distractions that are going on and being projected all around the world through social media. I was also a victim many years ago when I was seeking to know the Lord well and deeper, and a friend led me to an occulted church. When I arrived and first met the leader with the Bible in his hands, I felt safe and said, yes, this is the place and prayer camp I want to stay at. Not until the midnight hours, they woke us all up in the camp and led us through the forest to a river to bathe and perform incantations and call on dark spirits. Immediately, I realized something was wrong, and I sought to leave. They warned me that I would die in the forest on the way within that hour, but I said I would rather die than to live and serve those spirits. I prayed a simple prayer and said to the Lord, "I know you are not here, and I am leaving in your name. If I die, these people will mock you, but at least I will be with you," and I made it back home but was haunted by spirits every night until I met a woman of God Rev Diana who delivered me by the power of the Holy Ghost.

Thus says the Lord: "Stand in the ways and see and ask for the old paths, where the good way is, and walk in it; then you will find rest for your souls. But they said, we will not walk in it" (Jeremiah 6:16).

The ancient way of serving the Lord is still working because God is still the same yesterday, today, and forever.

It is my prayer that after you have read this book with the testimonies, your spirit is stirred up to take your relationship with Jesus to the next level, so you too can live life and live it abundantly.

If I was able to run to Jesus, I believe you can, too.

Printed in the USA
CPSIA information can be obtained
at www.ICGtesting.com
LVHW022017151024
793894LV00008B/221

9 798893 339130